A TEXT BOOK OF REMOTE SENSING, GIS AND GNSS

DR. SAILESH SAMANTA

Made with ♥ on the Notion Press Platform
www.notionpress.com

Contents

Foreword

The discipline of Geographic Information Science is a science that develops and manages graphic information systems infrastructure to address the problems related to geoscience and engineering. The three fundamental activities of geographic information science are: (i) Development and management of geographically referenced databases, (ii) Analysis and modeling of geographic data, and (iii) Development and integration of specific disciplines in remote sensing, photogrammetry, surveying, mapping and cartography, and technologies in geographic information systems, computing, and global positioning systems for the first two activities.

The discipline aims at integrating the emerging state-of-art technologies of data acquisition (remote sensing and digital photogrammetry), digital cartography and mapping, geographic information systems, Global Positioning System (GPS), electronic publishing, web, and multi-media cartography, and information technology.

The graduates are GIS professionals who will be basically GIS as well as CAD / CAM users and operators. Also, they will be involved in surveying and GIS data capture, data manipulation, data display, and production of quality output. All in all, the degree course will prepare students for GIS management positions. The course focuses more on GIS design, development, and management. Excellent employment opportunities for GIS graduates exist in the traditional sectors (surveying and mapping) and other areas such as education, engineering, agriculture, forestry, environmental science, legal arena, and business.

Dr. Sailesh Samanta

Associate Professor, GIS Section Head, Course Coordinator, B.Sc. in Geomatics (Distance Mode), Department of Survey and Land Studies, The PNG University of Technology, Lae-411, Morobe, PNG

Date: 2023

Preface

This text book is designed to be used for the students as an introductory course in Remote Sensing, Geographical Information System, Surveying, Geomatics, and Property Studies. There are three themes in this text book, such as Remote Sensing (RS) and its kindred technologies, namely Geographical Information System (GIS), Global Positioning System (GPS)/Global Navigation Satellite System (GNSS).

Remote sensing is the science (and to some extent, art) of acquiring information about the Earth's surface without actually being in contact with it. This is done by sensing and recording reflected or emitted energy and processing, analyzing, and applying that information. Satellite remote sensing is being conducted from space, where a sensor is stationed in a satellite to scan or collect pictures/information of the Earth's surface features.

A geographic information system (GIS) is a system of hardware, software, and procedures designed to support the capture, store, manage, manipulate, analyse, and display of spatially referenced data for solving complex planning and management problems. Work on GIS began in the late 1950s, but the first GIS software came only in the late 1970s from the lab of the ESRI. GIS has been important for many professionals, such as foresters, urban planners, and geologists, who have recognized the importance of spatial dimensions in organising and analysing information such as natural resource management, land use planning, natural hazards, transportation, health care, public services, market area analysis, and urban planning. It has also become a necessary tool for government agencies of all levels for routine operations.

Global Navigation Satellite System is the terminology given to all constellations of Satellites for positioning, navigation, and time on many applications on and above the Earth's surface. GNSS includes the Major universal satellite systems and as well the Regional/National Satellite Systems that were mainly produced to assist the GPS satellite system. The system allows small electronic receivers to determine their location to high precision using time signals transmitted along a line of sight by radio from satellites.

To become RS/GIS/GPS/GNSS professionals, students must be familiar with the technology as well as the basic concepts that drive the technology.

This text book will provide students with an overarching introduction to remote sensing (RS), geographical information system (GIS), and global navigational satellite system (GNSS) and their core components and utilities in terms of natural and manmade resources management.

Dr. Sailesh Samanta

Date: 2023

Acknowledgements

The authors are thankful to the Papua New Guinea University of Technology (PNGUNITECH) and to the Department of Surveying and Land Studies and the Department of open and distance learning for their guidance and instructions.

I take this privilege to express my heartfelt gratefulness to Dr. Dilip Kumar Pal, Ex-Professor and Head, Department of Surveying and Land Studies, the Papua New Guinea University of Technology for his continuous encouragement and able guidance throughout the length of his engagement with the department.

Thanks to Prof. Jacob Babarinde, Ex-Professor and Head, Department of Surveying and Land Studies, the Papua New Guinea University of Technology for his continuous encouragement to write this book in time.

Last, but not least I would like to pay my heartiest and special thanks to my beloved wife, Babita Palsamanta for her moral support from day one to this day of completion of my work.

Prologue

The text book is laid out in twelve (12) chapters. Chapter 1 deals with the general introduction of remote sensing, stages of remote sensing, electromagnetic radiation, and the electromagnetic spectrum. Chapter 2 describes satellite system and their type, and orbital characteristics for remote sensing purposes. Chapter 3 explains how incoming electromagnetic radiation interacts with the atmosphere and earth's surface features. Chapter 4 deliberates about the recognition of Earth's surface features based on three fundamental energy interactions with the feature. Chapter 5 gives details on the capabilities of remote sensing sensors: the resolution of a sensor and its type; types of remote sensing, type of scanning system and data rate of a sensor, and examples of remote satellite images and applications of remote sensing. Chapter 6 introduces the concept of GIS, components of GIS, and the type of Geospatial data. Chapter 7 deliberates about spatial data model: raster data structure/model. Chapter 8 explains vector data structure and vector data model and the advantages of Raster and Vector data model. Chapter 9 is deals with non-spatial data or attribute data, attribute data models, and applications of GIS. Chapter 10 emphasizes Global navigation satellite systems (GNSS), which is the constellations of major universal Satellite system and their positioning. Chapter 11 gives the real scenario of different Components of the Global Positioning System (GPS), like space segment, control segments, and user segments. Chapter 12 explains the basic principles of core functions of GPS and Differential GPS.

CHAPTER ONE

Introduction of Remote Sensing

Learning Outcomes

On completion of this chapter students will be able to:

1. Understand the gamut of remote sensing
2. Describe various stages of remote sensing
3. Recognize energy source and radiation principles

1.1 Concept of Remote Sensing and its Definition

Remote sensing is a general term that describes the action of obtaining information about an object with a sensor that is physically separated from the object. Such sensors rely upon the detection of energy emitted from or reflected by the object. Two common examples of remote sensing are human vision, which relies on the detection of reflected light, and sonar, which detects sound waves. In the context of micro BRIAN, remote sensing is primarily concerned with deriving information about the Earth's surface using an elevated platform. Remotely sensed data provide an ideal 'view' of the Earth for various resource inventory and monitoring studies. As such, remote sensing has saved considerable effort and cost in terms of traditional surveying methods and provides a consistent base for the extrapolation and interpolation of ground reconnaissance data.

Remote sensing is the science of making (information) inferences about the object from measurement, at a distance without coming into physical contact with the object under study. Remote sensing refers to any method, which can be used together with information about an object without actually coming in contact with it. In this context, any force field acoustic, gravity, magnetic, or electromagnetic called is used for remote sensing. Remote sensing employed sensing the earth's surface from space by making use of the properties of the electromagnetic wave emitted, reflected, or diffracted by the sensed object for the purpose of improving natural resource management land use, and the protection of the environment.

The definition of remote sensing can be expressed as "Remote sensing is the science (and to some extent, art) of acquiring information about the Earth's surface without actually being in contact with it. This is done by sensing and recording reflected or emitted energy and processing, analyzing, and applying that information" (CCRS, 2009).

1.2 Stages of Remote Sensing

In much of remote sensing, the process involves an interaction between incident radiation and the targets of interest. This is exemplified by the use of imaging systems where the following seven stages/elements are involved. However, that remote sensing also involves the sensing of an emitted energy and the use of non-imaging sensors.

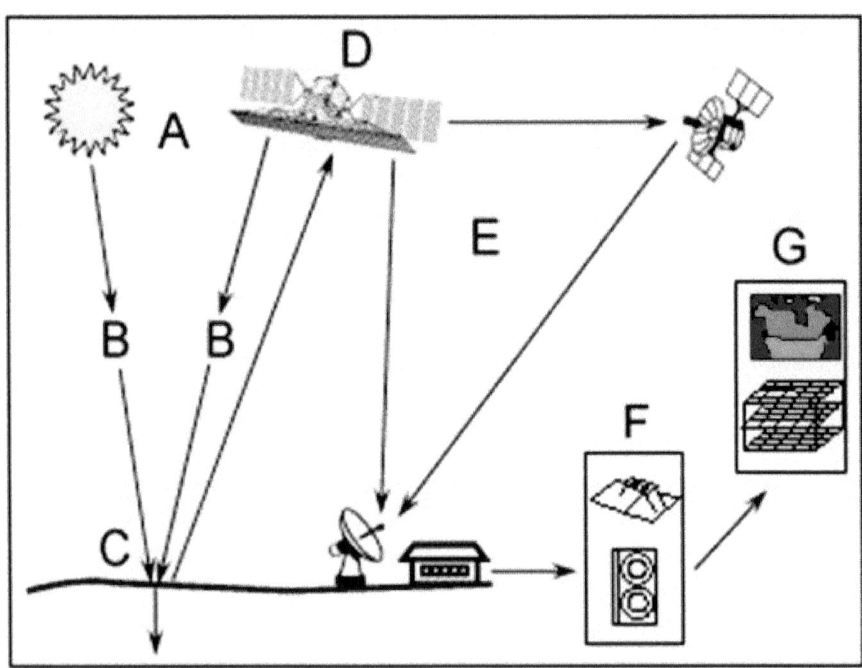

Figure 1.1 Stages of Remote Sensing

A. Energy Source or Illumination: The first requirement for remote sensing is to have an energy source that illuminates or provides electromagnetic energy to the target of interest.

B. Radiation and the Atmosphere: As the energy travels from its source to the target, it will come in contact with and interact with the atmosphere it passes through. This interaction may take place a second time as the energy travels from the target to the sensor.

C. Interaction with the Target: Once the energy makes its way to the target through the atmosphere, it interacts with the target depending on the properties of both the target and the radiation.

D. Recording of Energy by the Sensor: After the energy has been scattered by, or emitted from the target, we require a sensor (remote - not in contact with the target) to collect and record the electromagnetic radiation.

E. Transmission, Reception, and Processing: The energy recorded by the sensor has to be transmitted, often in electronic form, to a receiving and processing station where the data are processed into an image (hardcopy and/or digital).

F. Interpretation and Analysis: The processed image is interpreted, visually and/or digitally or electronically, to extract information about the target which was illuminated.

G. Application: The final element of the remote sensing process is achieved when we apply the information we have been able to extract from the imagery about the target in order to better understand it, reveal some new information, or assist in solving a particular problem.

These seven stages/elements comprise the satellite remote sensing process from beginning to end.

1.3 Electromagnetic Radiation

The first requirement for remote sensing is to have an energy source to illuminate the target (unless the sensed energy is being emitted by the target). This energy is in the form of electromagnetic radiation (Lillesand et al, 2015).

All electromagnetic radiation has fundamental properties and behaves in predictable ways according to the basics of wave theory. Electromagnetic radiation consists of an electrical field (E) which varies in magnitude in a direction perpendicular to the direction in which the radiation is traveling, and a magnetic field (M) oriented at right angles to the electrical field. Both these fields travel at the speed of light (c) (Figure 1.2).

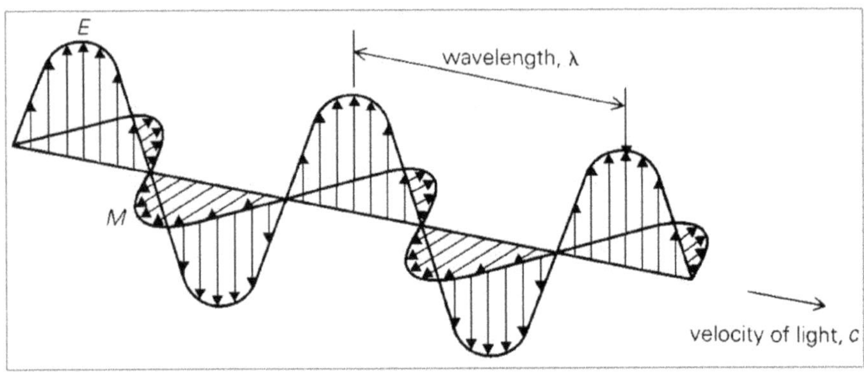

Figure 1.2 Electromagnetic radiation

Electromagnetic waves travel with a velocity c = 2.99792458 x 10^8 m/s ($3x10^8$ m/s) in the form of combined electric and magnetic fields. All electromagnetic waves travel through space at the same speed, commonly known as the **speed of light (c)**. An electromagnetic wave is characterized by a **frequency (f)** and a **wavelength** (λ). These two quantities are related to the speed of light by the equation (CCRS, 2009).

Speed of light (c) = frequency (f) x wavelength (λ)

The frequency (and hence, the wavelength) of an electromagnetic wave depends on its source. We encounter a wide range of frequencies in our physical world, ranging from the low frequency of the electric waves generated by the power transmission lines to the very high frequency of the gamma rays originating from the atomic nuclei. This wide frequency range of electromagnetic waves constitutes the **Electromagnetic Spectrum**. Therefore, the two are inversely related to each other. The shorter the wavelength refers to the higher the frequency (Figure 1.3). The longer the wavelength refers the lower the frequency. Understanding the characteristics of electromagnetic radiation in terms of its wavelength and frequency is crucial to understanding the information to be extracted from remote sensing data.

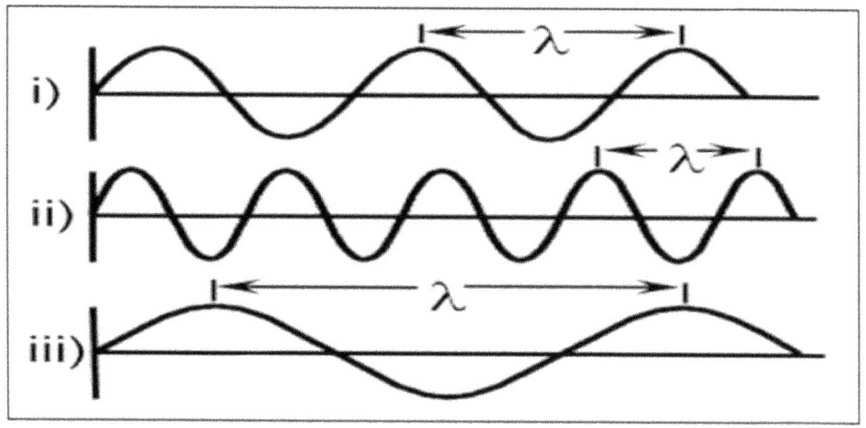

Figure 1.3 Relationship between wavelength and frequency

1.4 The Electromagnetic Spectrum

The electromagnetic spectrum ranges from shorter wavelengths (including gamma and x-rays) to longer wavelengths (including microwaves and broadcast radio waves). There are several regions of the electromagnetic spectrum which are useful for remote sensing (Campbell and Wynne, 2011). The electromagnetic spectrum can be divided into several wavelength (frequency) regions. The various wavelength regions of the electromagnetic spectrum are (Figure 1.4):

Radio Waves (10 cm to 10 km): The portion of the spectrum that is not interesting to remote sensing is the radio wave region from10 cm to 10 km wavelength. Thesc types of wavelengths are used for radio broadcasting and communication purposes.

Microwaves (1 mm to 1 m): The portion of the spectrum of more recent interest in remote sensing is the microwave region from about 1 mm to 1 m. This covers the longest wavelengths used for remote sensing. The microwaves are further divided into different frequency (wavelength) bands

- P band: 0.3 - 1 GHz (30 - 100 cm)
- L band: 1 - 2 GHz (15 - 30 cm)
- S band: 2 - 4 GHz (7.5 - 15 cm)
- C band: 4 - 8 GHz (3.8 - 7.5 cm)

- X band: 8 - 12.5 GHz (2.4 - 3.8 cm)
- Ku band: 12.5 - 18 GHz (1.7 - 2.4 cm)
- K band: 18 - 26.5 GHz (1.1 - 1.7 cm)
- Ka band: 26.5 - 40 GHz (0.75 - 1.1 cm)

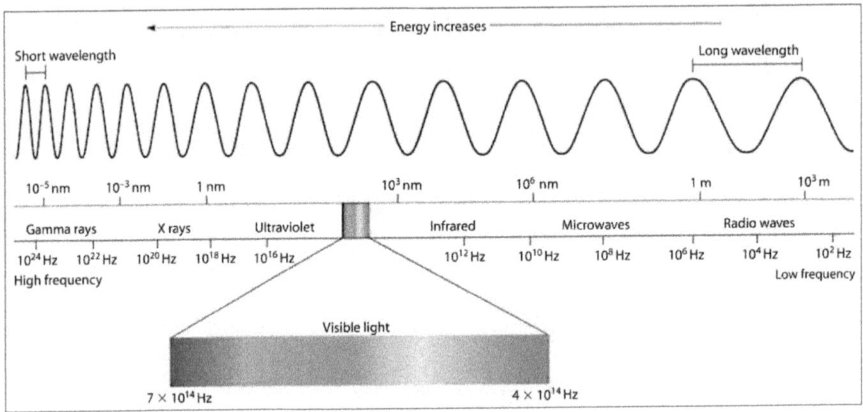

Figure 1.4 Electromagnetic Spectrum

Infrared (0.7 to 1 mm): The next portion of the spectrum of interest is the infrared (IR) region which covers the wavelength range from approximately 0.7 μm to 1 mm - more than 100 times as wide as the visible portion! The infrared region can be divided into two categories based on its radiation properties - the **reflected IR**, and the emitted or **thermal IR.** Radiation in the reflected IR region is used for remote sensing purposes in ways very similar to radiation in the visible portion. The reflected IR covers wavelengths from approximately 0.7 μm to 3.0 μm. The thermal IR region is quite different than the visible and reflected IR portions, as this energy is essentially the radiation that is emitted from the Earth's surface in the form of heat. The thermal IR covers wavelengths from approximately 3.0 μm to 15μm.

This region is further divided into the following bands:

- Near Infrared (NIR): 0.7 to 1.5 μm.
- Short Wavelength Infrared (SWIR): 1.5 to 3 μm.
- Mid Wavelength Infrared (MWIR): 3 to 8 μm.
- Long Wavelength Infrared (LWIR): 8 to 15 μm.

- Far Infrared (FIR): longer than 15 µm.

The NIR and SWIR also known as the *Reflected Infrared* are the main infrared component of the solar radiation reflected from the earth's surface. The MWIR and LWIR are the *Thermal Infrared.*

Visible Light (0.4 to 0.7 µm): The visible wavelengths cover a range from approximately 0.4 to 0.7 µm. The longest visible wavelength is red and the shortest is violet. The various colour components of the visible spectrum fall roughly within the following wavelength regions:

- Red: 0.620 - 0.7 µm,
- Orange: 0.592 - 0.620 µm
- Yellow: 0.578 - 0.592 µm
- Green: 0.500 - 0.578 µm
- Blue: 0.446 - 0.500 µm
- Violet: 0.4 - 0.446 µm

Blue, **green**, and **red** are the **primary colours** or wavelengths of the visible spectrum. The visible portion of this radiation can be shown in its component colours when sunlight is passed through a prism, which bends the light in differing amounts according to wavelength (Figure 1.5).

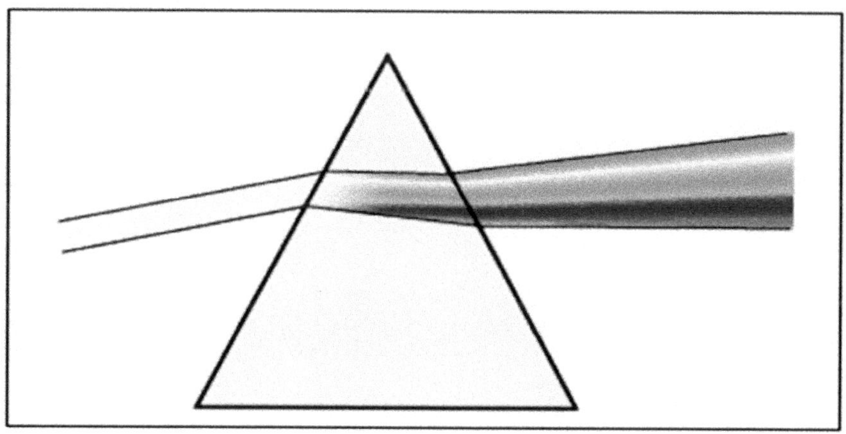

Figure 1.5 Effects after light passes through a prism

Ultraviolet (0.003 to 0.4µm): For most purposes, the ultraviolet or UV portion of the spectrum has the shortest wavelengths which are practical for remote sensing. This radiation is just beyond the violet portion of the visible wavelengths, hence its name. Some Earth surface materials, primarily rocks, and minerals fluoresce or emit visible light when illuminated by UV radiation.

X-Rays and Gamma Rays (smaller wavelengths than Ultraviolet): X-rays are entirely absorbed by the Earth's atmosphere and are not available for remote sensing, but are useful in medical science. Gamma rays consist of the shortest wavelength electromagnetic waves and so impart the highest photon energy and are not available for remote sensing.

CHAPTER TWO

SATELLITE SYSTEM AND ORBITAL CHARACTERISTICS

Learning Outcomes

On completion of this chapter students will be able to:

1. Understand the concept of satellite and its type
2. Illustrate Kepler's law of planetary motion
3. Explain the fundamentals behind the stabilization of a satellite in the orbit

2.1 Concept of Satellite

A body that moves around the mother planate in its fixed path is called a satellite. A satellite may be classified as a manmade or heavenly body orbiting under the influence of gravity around the mother planet. Satellites may be of two types, namely (a) natural satellites and (b) arterial satellites. Natural satellites are naturally formed planate and move around their mother planate in a fixed path like Moon is a natural satellite of the Earth. Artificial satellites are manmade satellites that launch from the earth's surface and got a fixed path to move around the earth. IRS and LANDSAT are artificial satellites.

2.2 Satellite Orbits

The path followed by a satellite is referred to as its orbit. A satellite follows a generally elliptical orbit around the earth in accordance with three Keplerian laws (Russell, 1964). There are mainly two types of satellite orbit, namely Geostationary orbit and the Sun-synchronous orbit. The time taken by a satellite to complete one revolution through the orbit is called the orbital period. The satellite traces out a path on the earth's surface, called its ground track, as it moves across the sky. As the earth below is rotating, the satellite traces out a different path on the ground in each subsequent cycle. Sun-synchronous remote sensing satellites are often launched into special orbits such that the satellite repeats its path after a fixed time interval. This time interval is called the repeat cycle of the satellite.

2.2.1 Geostationary Orbits

If a satellite follows an orbit parallel to the equator in the same direction as the earth's rotation and within the same period of 24 hours, the satellite will appear stationary with respect to the earth's surface.

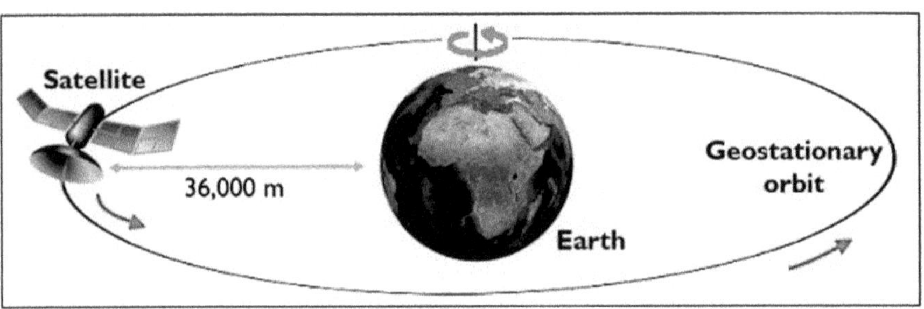

Figure 2.1 Geostationary Orbit and satellite

This orbit is a **geostationary** orbit (Figure 2.1). Satellites in the geostationary orbits are located at a high altitude of 36,000 km (Lillesand et al., 2015). These orbits enable a satellite to always view the same area on the earth. A large area of the earth can also be covered by a satellite. The geostationary orbits are commonly used by **meteorological satellites.** Due to their high altitude, some geostationary weather satellites can monitor weather and cloud patterns covering an entire hemisphere of the Earth.

2.2.2 Sun Synchronous Orbits

A **near-polar orbit** is one with the orbital plane inclined at a small angle with respect to the earth's rotation axis. A satellite following a properly designed near-polar orbit passes close to the poles and is able to cover nearly the whole earth's surface in a repeat cycle. Earth observation satellites usually follow the sun-synchronous orbits (Figure 2.2). A sun-synchronous orbit is a near-polar orbit whose altitude is such that the satellite will always pass over a location at given latitude at the same **local solar time** called local sun time. In this way, the same solar illumination condition (except for seasonal variation) can be achieved for the images of a given location taken by the satellite (Campbell and Wynne, 2011).

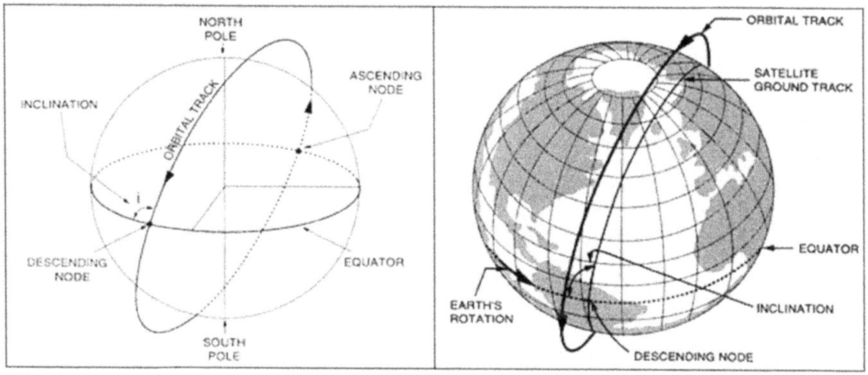

Figure 2.2 Near-polar or sun-synchronous orbit/satellite

Most of the remote sensing satellite platforms today are in near-polar orbits, which means that the satellite travels northwards on one side of the Earth and then toward the south pole in the second half of its orbit. These are called ascending and descending passes, respectively. If the orbit is also sun-synchronous, the ascending pass is most likely on the shadowed side of the Earth while the descending pass is on the sunlit side. Sensors recording reflected solar energy only image the surface on a descending pass when solar illumination is available.

2.3 Kepler's Law of Planetary Motion (1609-1666)

Johannes Kepler proposed three laws of planetary motion. He described the motion of planets in a sun-centered solar system. Kepler's efforts to explain these three laws are still considered an accurate description of the motion of any planet and any satellite. These laws of planetary motion can be stated (Russell, 1964) as follows:

2.3.1 Kepler's first law: *"All planets move in elliptical orbits, with the sun at one focus"* (Russell, 1964). *[Each satellite describes an elliptic orbit with the earth at the focus]*. Planets are orbiting the Sun in a path described as an ellipse. An ellipse is a special curve in which the sum of the distances from every point on the curve to two other points is a constant. The two other points are known as the foci of the ellipse. The "Perihelion" point along the ellipse (planet's orbit) is the closest position of the Earth to the sun and the "aphelion" is furthest from the sun.

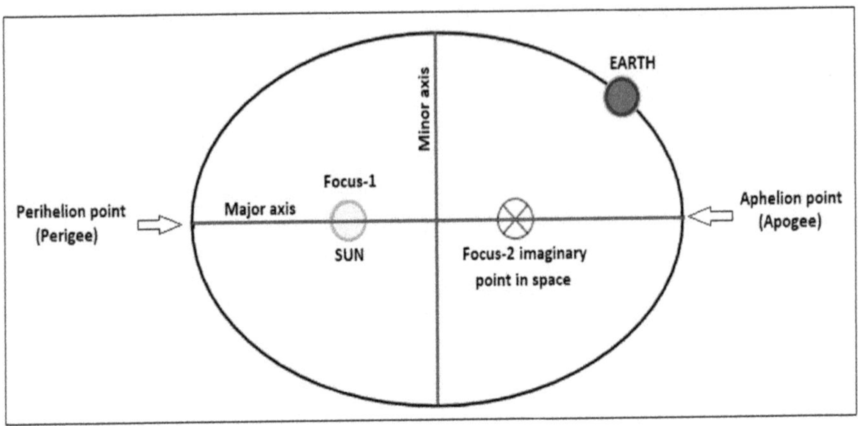

Figure 2.3 Schematics of the elliptical orbit

Apogee Position is the point when the distance between the satellite and the Earth is higher than any other position. The distance between the satellite and the center of Earth is called apogee distance.

Perigee Position is the point when the distance between satellite and earth is low. The distance between the satellite and the Earth is called perigee distance.

Major Axis: The Sum of the apogee and perigee distance is called as major axis.

(Note As per figure 2.4: Earth radius {R = 6378 km} should be added with each distance while calculating the major axis if the height of the satellite is being considered from the surface of the Earth {Mean Sea Level})

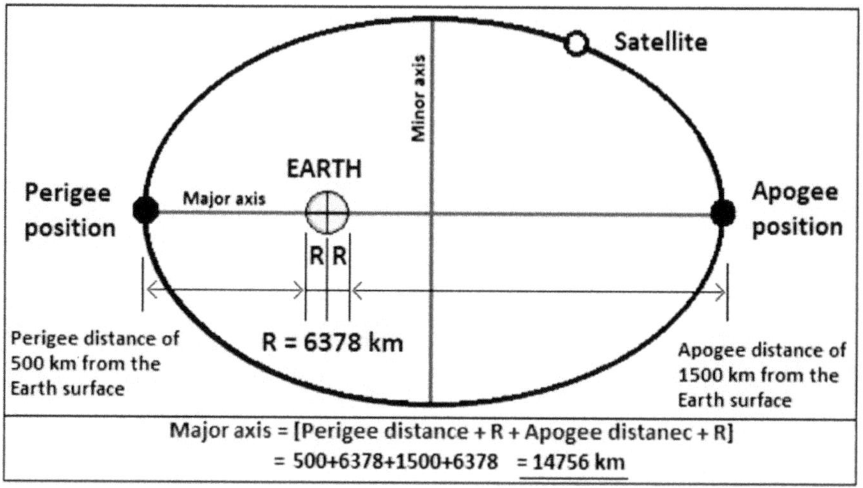

Figure 2.4 Major axes calculation process

Semi-major Axis: Mean distance of a satellite from the earth is called Semi-major distance.

Minor Axis: The minor axis is the longest line segment perpendicular to the major axis.

2.3.2 Kepler's second law: *The line joining the planet to the sun sweeps out equal areas in equal intervals of time* (Russell, 1964). *[The line joining the satellite and the center of the earth, sweeps out equal areas in equal intervals of time].* The Second law describes the speed at which any given planet or satellite will move while orbiting the Sun or the Earth. The speed at which any planet or satellite moves through space is constantly changing. A planet/satellite move fastest when it is closest to the Sun/Earth and slowest when it is furthest (Figute 2.5).

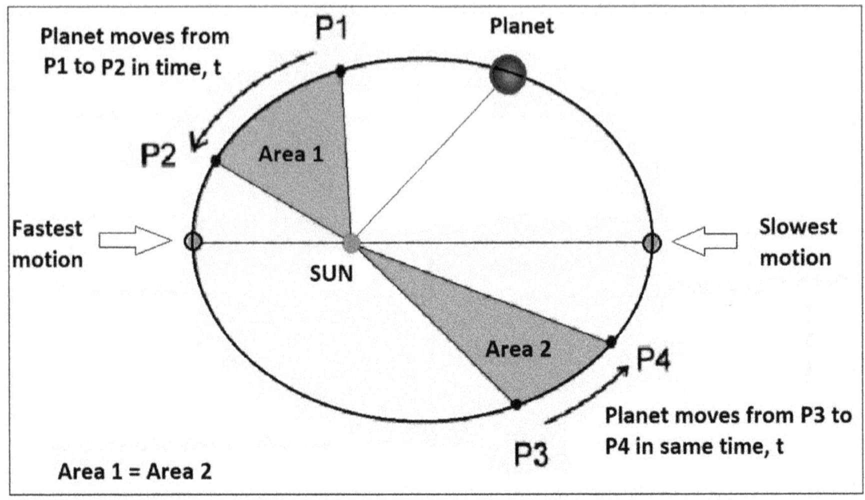

Figure 2.5 Schematics of Kepler's 2nd law

2.3.3 Kepler's third law: "*The Square of the period of a planet is proportional to the cube of its mean distance from the sun (Semi-major axis)*" (Russell, 1964). *[The square of the period of a satellite is proportional to the cube of the mean distance from the center of the earth]*. The third law makes a comparison between the motion characteristics of different planets or satellites.

$$P^2 \infty H^3$$

Or

$$P^2=(1/g)\ (2\pi/R)^2(H)^3$$

Where, P= Period of satellite in orbit, H= Height of satellite from the earth center, H= (R+h)

R= Radius of the Earth (6378 km), h= Height of satellite from Earth surface, g= Gravity (0.00981km/s²)

Calculation of Period: A satellite is situated at a height of 904 km from the earth's surface. Calculate the period of the satellite.

Solution: $\mathbf{P^2= (1/g)(2\pi/R)^2(H)^3}$

$P^2= (1/0.00981km/s^2) \times (2\pi/6378km)^2 \times (6378 + 904km)^3$

$P^2= 38200911.3\ s^2$

$P = \sqrt{38200911.3\ s^2}$

$P = 6180.69\ s$

$= 103.01$ minutes

2.4 How the Satellite stabilized in the orbit?

With the help of escape velocity (11.2 km/sec), the satellite moves away from the atmosphere as well as from the gravitational force. After launching the satellite it gets a fixed path/orbit to move around the mother planate by tangential force (8km/sec). Due to the centripetal and centrifugal force of the satellite in the orbit (Figure 2.6), the satellites become stabilized (Curtis, 2010).

Centripetal force: It is a force by which the satellite pulls towards the earth's center (Curtis, 2010).

$$P=G(MeMs/D^2)$$

Where, P= Centripetal Force, G= Gravity, Me= Mass of Earth, Ms=Mass of satellite, D=Distance of the satellite from Earth center (R+h)

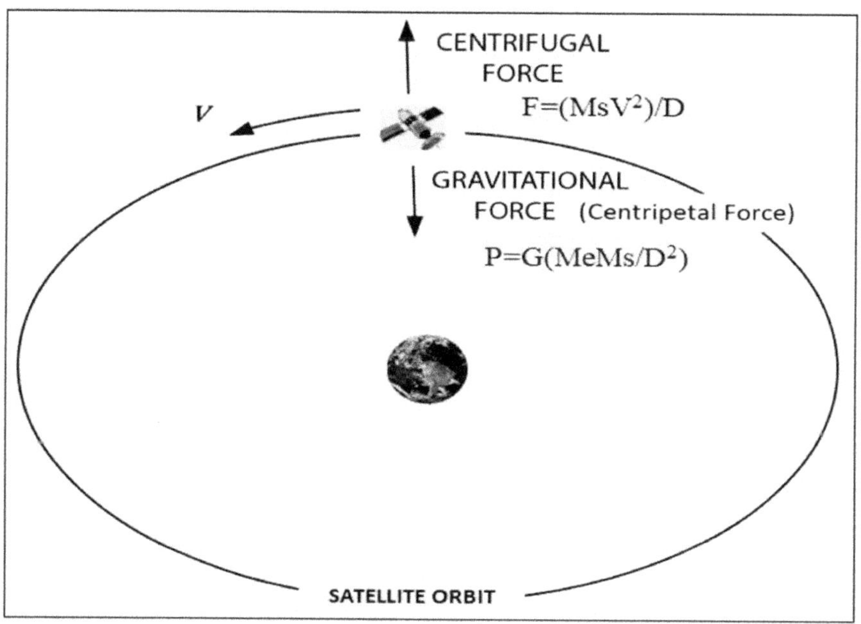

Figure 2.6 Centripetal and centrifugal force

Centrifugal force: It is the force by which a satellite pushes away from the center of the earth against the gravitational force (Chraibi et al., 2010).

$$F= (MsV2)/D$$

Where, F= Centrifugal Force, V = Velocity, Ms = Mass of satellite, D = Distance of satellite from Earth center (R+h)

The satellite will be stabilized if these two forces become equal, ***Centripetal force (P) = Centrifugal force (F) which can be expressed as:***

$G(MeMs/D^2) = (MsV^2)/D$

Or $GMe/D = V^2$

Or $V^2 = GMe/D$

Or $V= \sqrt{(GMe/D)}$ $\sqrt{GMe} = 631$ km/sec

Or $V= 631/\sqrt{D}$

Calculation of velocity: A satellite is situated at a height of 904 km from the earth's surface. Calculate the velocity of the satellite.

Solution: $V= 631/\sqrt{D}$

Where-V=Velocity, D=the distance of satellite from Earth center (R+h),

$V= 631/\sqrt{(6378+904)}$ km/sec

$V= 7.39$ km/sec

The average velocity of the satellite in the orbit is 7.39 km/sec

CHAPTER THREE

INTERACTION OF INCOMING ELECTROMAGNETIC RADIATION

Learning Outcomes

On completion of this chapter students will be able to:

1. Illustrate the role of the atmosphere in remote sensing
2. Explain atmospheric scattering and atmospheric windows
3. Understand how energy interacts with earth's surface features

3.1 Interactions of incoming EMR with the Atmosphere

As the energy travels from its source to the target, it will come in contact with and interact with the atmosphere it passes through. This interaction may take place a second time as the energy travels from the target to the sensor.

Before radiation used for remote sensing reaches the Earth's surface it has to travel through some distance from the Earth's atmosphere. Particles and gases in the atmosphere can affect incoming light and radiation. These effects are caused by the mechanisms of scattering and absorption.

3.1.1 Scattering

Scattering occurs when particles or large gas molecules present in the atmosphere interact with and the electromagnetic radiation to be redirected from its original path (Figure 3.1). How much scattering takes place depends on several factors including the wavelength of the radiation, the abundance of particles or gases, and the distance the radiation travels through the atmosphere (Campbell and Wynne, 2011).

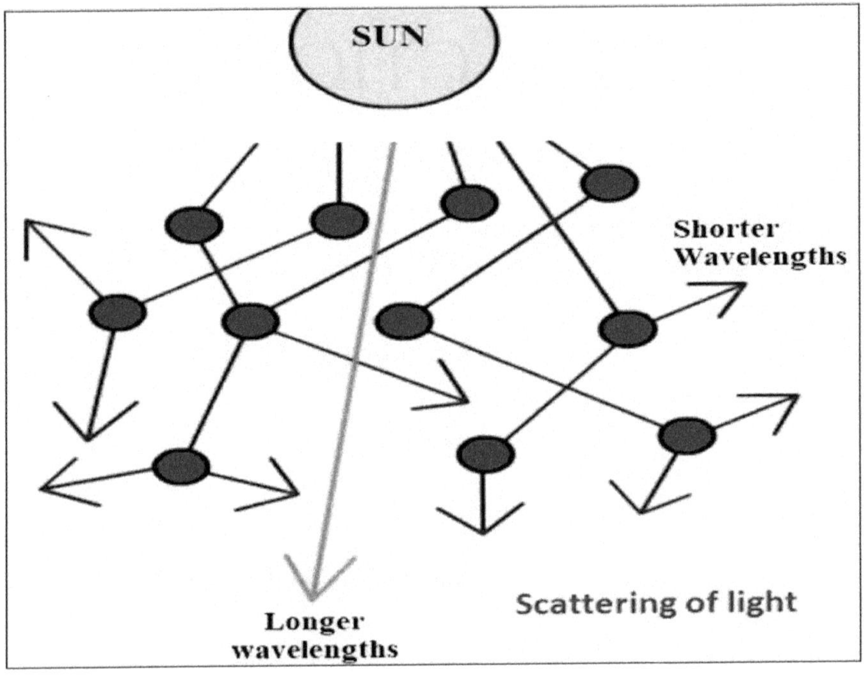

Figure 3.1 Incident energy and scattering in the atmosphere

There are three (3) types of scattering that take place in the atmosphere, namely (a) Rayleigh, (b) Mie and (c) Non-selective scattering.

Rayleigh scattering: Rayleigh scattering occurs when particles are very small compared to the wavelength of the radiation. These could be particles such as small specks of dust or nitrogen and oxygen molecules. Rayleigh scattering causes shorter wavelengths of energy to be scattered much more than longer wavelengths. Rayleigh scattering is the dominant scattering mechanism in the upper atmosphere (CCRS, 2009). A blue sky is a manifestation of Rayleigh scattering (Lillesand et al., 2015). As sunlight passes through the atmosphere, the shorter wavelengths (i.e. blue) of the visible spectrum are scattered more than the other (longer) visible wavelengths (Figure 3.2). Rayleigh scattering also produces red sunsets and sunrises.At sunrise and sunset, the light has to travel farther through the atmosphere than at midday and the scattering of the shorter wavelengths is more complete; this leaves a greater proportion of the longer wavelengths (Red) to penetrate the atmosphere and reached our eye.

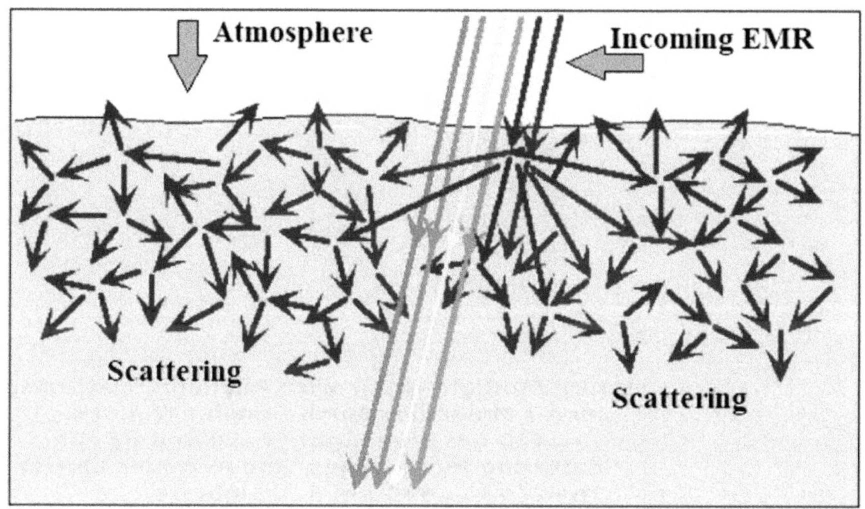

Figure 3.2 Rayleigh scattering (Blue light scattering)

Mie scattering: Mie scattering occurs when the particles are just about the same size as the wavelength of the radiation. Dust, pollen, smoke, and water vapors are common causes of Mie scattering which tends to affect longer wavelengths than those affected by Rayleigh scattering (Figure 3.3). Mie scattering occurs mostly in the lower portions of the atmosphere where larger particles are more abundant and dominates when cloud conditions are overcast (CCRS, 2009).

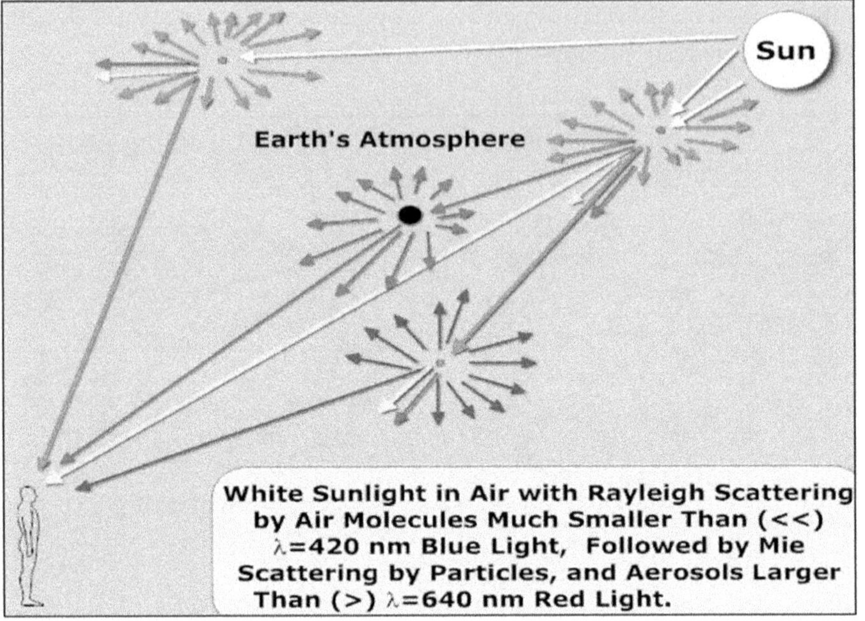

Figure 3.3 Rayleigh vs Mie scattering

Nonselective scattering: The final scattering mechanism of importance is called ***nonselective scattering***. This occurs when the particles are much larger than the wavelength of the radiation. Water droplets and large dust particles can cause this type of scattering. Nonselective scattering gets its name from the fact that all wavelengths are scattered about equally. In the visible wavelengths, equal quantities of blue, green, and red light are scattered; hence fog and clouds appear white (Lillesand et al., 2015) (Figure 3.4).

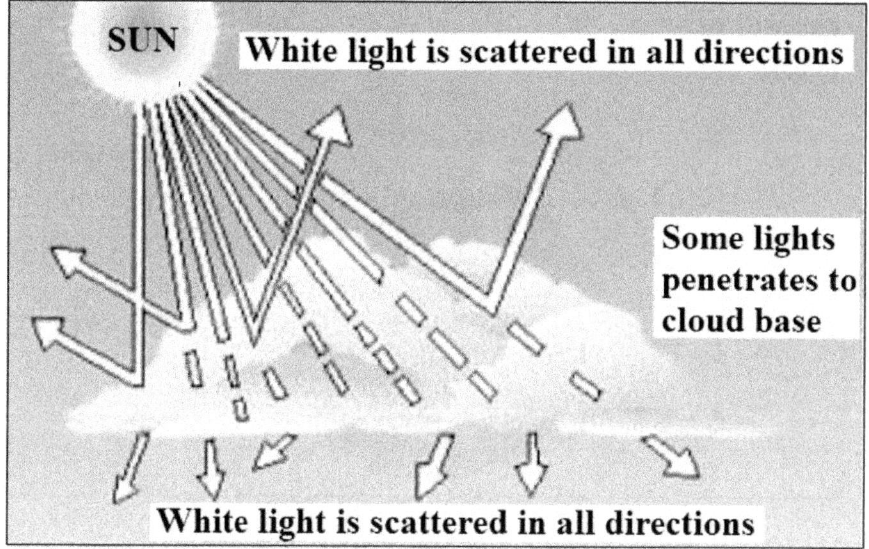

Figure 3.4 Non-selective scattering

3.1.2 Absorption

Absorption is the other main mechanism at work when electromagnetic radiation interacts with the atmosphere. In contrast to scattering, this phenomenon causes molecules in the atmosphere to absorb energy at various wavelengths. Ozone, carbon dioxide, and water vapour are the three main atmospheric constituents that absorb radiation (CCRS, 2009) (Figure 3.5).

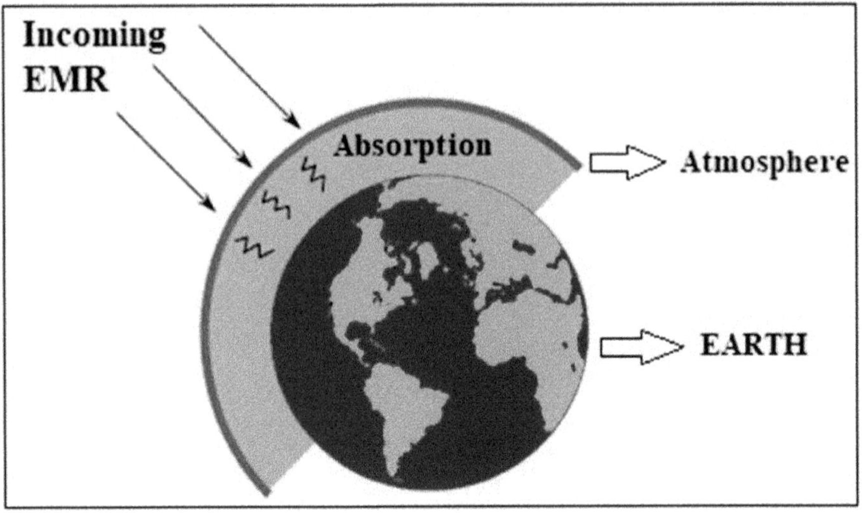

Figure 3.5 Atmosphere and absorption

Ozone serves to absorb the harmful (to most living things) ultraviolet radiation from the sun. Without this protective layer in the atmosphere, our skin would burn when exposed to sunlight.

Carbon dioxide is referred to as a greenhouse gas. This is because it tends to absorb radiation strongly in the far infrared portion of the spectrum - that is associated with thermal heating - which serves to trap this heat inside the atmosphere (CCRS, 2009). Water vapour in the atmosphere absorbs much of the incoming long-wave infrared and short-wave microwave radiation (between 22mm and 1mm). The presence of water vapour in the lower atmosphere varies greatly from location to location and at different times of the year. For example, the air mass above a desert would have very little water vapour to absorb energy, while the tropics would have high concentrations of water vapour (i.e. high humidity) (CCRS, 2009).

Because these gases absorb electromagnetic energy in very specific regions of the spectrum, they influence where (in the spectrum) we can "look" for remote sensing purposes. Those areas of the spectrum which are not severely influenced by atmospheric absorption and thus, are useful to remote sensors are called ***atmospheric windows*** (Figure 3.6).

By comparing the characteristics of the two most common energy/radiation sources (the sun and the earth) with the atmospheric windows available to us, we can define those wavelengths that we can use most effectively for remote sensing. The visible portion of the spectrum, to which our eyes are most sensitive, corresponds to both an atmospheric window and the peak energy level of the sun. Note also that heat energy emitted by the Earth corresponds to a window around 10 mm in the thermal IR portion of the spectrum, while the large window at wavelengths beyond 1 mm is associated with the microwave region (CCRS, 2009).

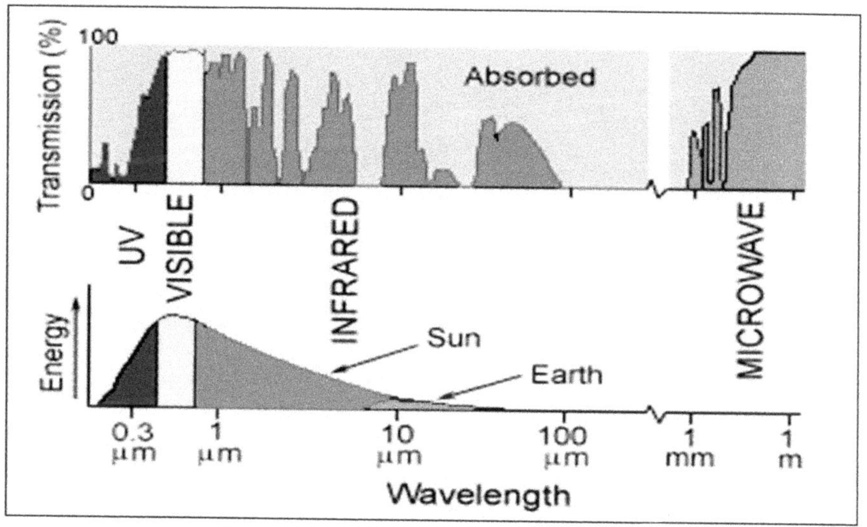

Figure 3.6 Atmospheric windows

Now that we understand how electromagnetic energy makes its journey from its source to the surface (and it is a difficult journey, as you can see) we will next examine what happens to that radiation when it does arrive at the Earth's surface.

3.2 Interactions of incoming EMR with the Target

Radiation that is not absorbed or scattered in the atmosphere can reach and interact with the Earth's surface. There are three (3) forms of interaction that can take place when energy strikes or is incident (I) upon the surface. These are absorption (A), transmission (T), and reflection (R) (Lillesand et al., 2015). The total incident energy will interact with the surface in one or more of these three ways (Figure 3.7).

EI(l) = ER(l) + EA(l) + ET(l)

Where,

EI (l) = incident energy in a particular wavelength (l)

ER (l) = energy reflected in a particular wavelength (l)

EA (l) = energy absorbed in a particular wavelength (l)

ET (l) = energy transmitted in a particular wavelength (l)

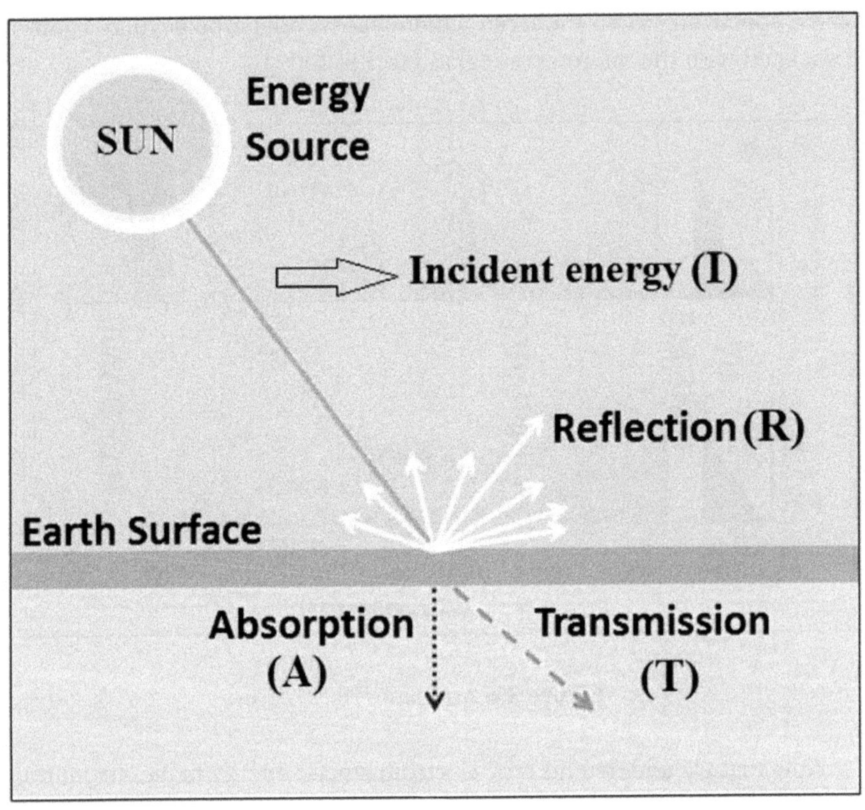

Figure 3.7 Interaction of incident energy with Earth surface features

The proportions of each interaction will depend on the wavelength of the energy and the material and condition of the feature. Absorption (A) occurs when radiation (energy) is absorbed into the target while transmission (T) occurs when radiation passes through a target. Reflection (R) occurs when radiation "bounces" off the target and is redirected. In remote sensing, we are most interested in measuring the radiation reflected from targets. We refer to two types of reflection, which represent the two extreme ends of the way in which energy is reflected from a target: **specular reflection** and **diffuse reflection** (CCRS, 2009).

When a surface is smooth we get a specular or mirror-like reflection where all (or almost all) of the energy is directed away from the surface in a single direction. Diffuse reflection occurs when the surface is rough and the energy is reflected almost uniformly in all directions. Most earth surface features lie somewhere between perfectly specular or perfectly diffuse reflectors.

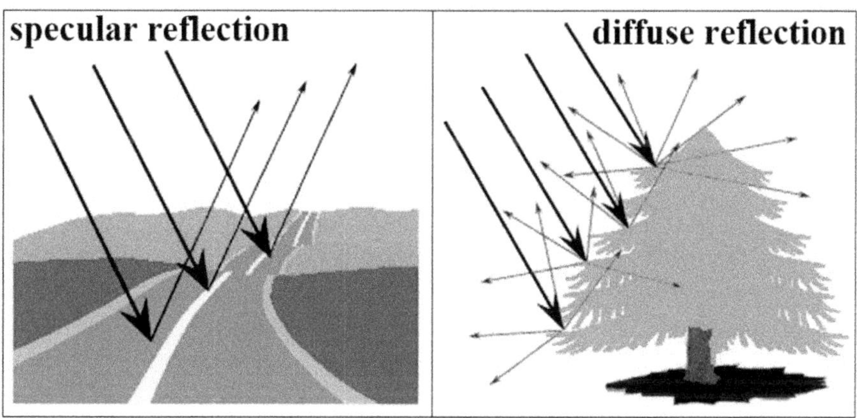

Figure 3.8 Specular and diffuse reflection

Whether a particular target reflects specularly or diffusely, or somewhere in between, depends on the surface roughness of the feature *in comparison to the wavelength of the incoming radiation.* If the wavelengths are much smaller than the surface variations or the particle sizes that make up the surface, the diffuse reflection will dominate [condition is surface roughness >$^1/_8$]. For example, fine-grained sand would appear fairly smooth to long wavelength microwaves but would appear quite rough to the visible wavelengths (CCRS, 2009).

The reflectance characteristics may be quantified by measuring the portion of the incident energy that is reflected. The measurement is done as a function of wavelength and is referred to as the spectral reflectance - Rl and it is mathematically expressed as (Lillesand et al., 2015):

$$Rl = [\ ER(l) / EI(l)\ ] * 100$$

A graph of the spectral reflectance of an object as a function of wavelength is termed a spectral reflectance curve. This curve gives an insight into the spectral characteristics of an object and helps in choosing the appropriate wavelength regions for a particular application (Lillesand et al., 2015).

CHAPTER FOUR

RECOGNITION OF EARTH'S SURFACE FEATURES

Learning Outcomes

On completion of this chapter students will be able to:

1. Understand the concept of spectral signature curve
2. Assess different surface features based on reflectance pattern

4.1 Introduction

When electromagnetic energy is incident on any given earth's surface feature, three fundamental energy interactions with the feature are possible – Absorption, Reflection and Transmission. Broadly speaking, Remote Sensing is concerned with detecting and recording electromagnetic radiation from target areas in the field of view of the sensor instrument. Electro-magnetic energy sensors are being operated from air-borne or space-borne platforms to assist in inventorying, mapping and monitoring of earth resources. These sensors emit and reflect electromagnetic energy, which is analyzed to provide information about the resources under investigation (Campbell and Wynne, 2011).

Visible light is only one of many forms of electromagnetic energy. Radio waves, heat, ultraviolet rays and X-rays are other familiar forms. When the energy is incident on any given earth surface feature, three fundamental energy interactions with the feature are possible. Various fractions of the energy incident on the element are reflected, absorbed and/or transmitted.

Two points concerning this relationship should be noted. First, the proportion of energy reflected, absorbed and transmitted will vary for different earth features, depending on their material type and condition. These differences permit us to distinguish different features in an image. Second, the wavelength dependency means that, even within a given feature type, the proportion of reflected, absorbed and transmitted energy will vary at different wavelengths. Thus, two features may be indistinguishable in one spectral range and be very different in another wavelength band. Within the visible portion of the spectrum, their spectral variations result in the visual effect – called colour. For example, we call objects 'blue' when they reflect highly in the blue portion of the spectrum, 'green' when they reflect highly in the green spectral region and so on (Lillesand et al., 2015).

Because many remote sensing systems operate in the wavelength regions in which reflected energy predominates, the reflectance properties of the earth's features are very important. If we consider the energy balance relationship, the reflected energy is equal to the energy incident on a given feature reduced by the energy that is either absorbed or transmitted by the feature. The geometric manner in which an object reflects energy is also an important consideration. This factor is primarily a function of the surface roughness of the object. Specular reflectors are flat surfaces that manifest mirror-like reflections, where the angle of reflection equals the angle of incidence with respect to the singular normal that can be drawn at the point of incidence. Diffused (or Lambertian) reflectors are rough surfaces that reflect uniformly in all directions because of changing the direction of multiple normals emanating from the roughness of the surface. Most earth surface features are neither perfectly specular nor diffused reflectors. Their characteristics are somewhat in between the two extremes (Campbell and Wynne, 2011).

A graph of the spectral reflectance of an object as a function of wavelength is termed a spectral reflectance curve. The configuration of the spectral reflectance curve gives us insight into the spectral characteristics of an object and has a strong influence on the choice of wavelength region(s) in which remote sensing data are acquired for a particular application. Earth surface features of interest can be identified, mapped and studied on the basis of their spectral characteristics. The figure below shows a typical spectral reflectance curve of three basic types of earth features: healthy green vegetation, bare soil and clear lake water (Figure 4.1).

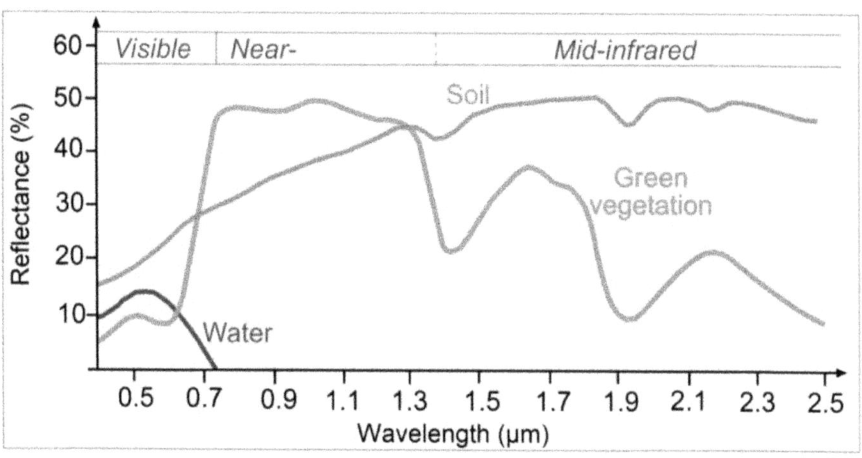

Figure 4.1 Reflectance of water, soil and vegetation at different wavelengths

4.2 Spatial reflectance curve for Vegetation

A chemical compound in leaves called chlorophyll strongly absorbs radiation in the red and blue wavelengths but reflects green wavelengths (Figure 4.2). Leaves appear "greenest" to us in the summer, when chlorophyll content is at its maximum. In autumn, there is less chlorophyll in the leaves, so there is less absorption and proportionately more reflection of the red wavelengths, making the leaves appear red or yellow (yellow is a combination of red and green wavelengths) (Campbell and Wynne, 2011). The internal structure of healthy leaves acts as excellent diffuse reflectors of near-infrared wavelengths. If our eyes were sensitive to near-infrared, trees would appear extremely bright to us at these wavelengths (Figure 4.2). In fact, measuring and monitoring the near-IR reflectance is one way that scientists can determine how healthy (or unhealthy) vegetation may be (CCRS, 2009).

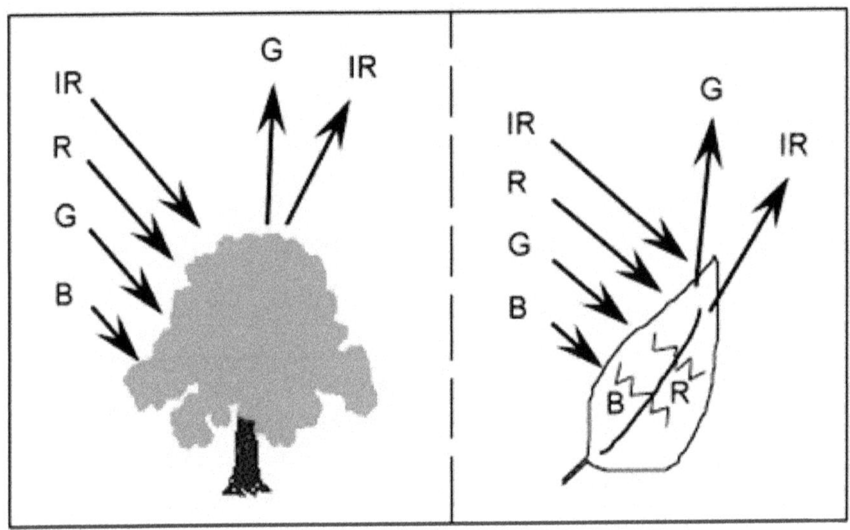

Figure 4.2 Reflectance pattern of a green tree/leaf

Figure 4.3 shows the mechanism of reflectance emanating from different points of the cross-section of a plant leaf.

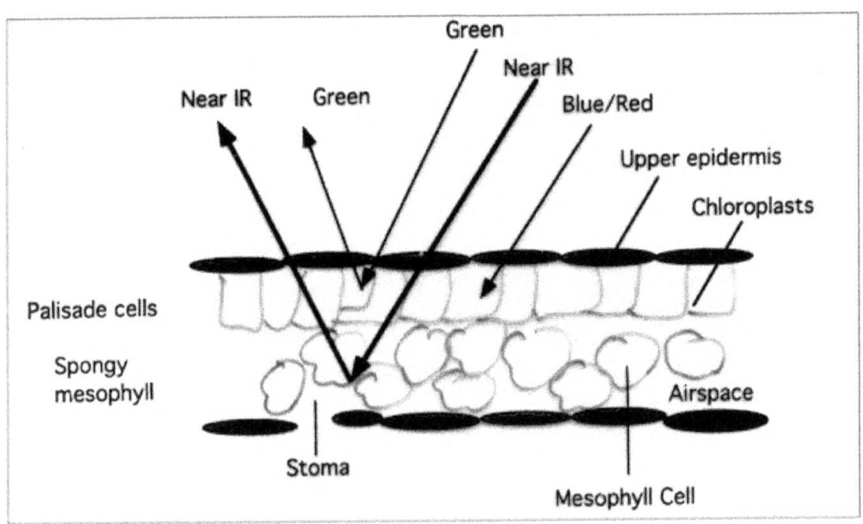

Figure 4.3 Mechanism of reflectance from a plant leaf

In summary green vegetation has a distinctive reflectance curve:

- Absorption in blue
- Reflection in green
- Absorption in red
- Strong reflection in NIR

Their reflectance patters are depended on:

i. VISIBLE- Pigment type/concentration and surface features: hairs, spines, veins, cuticular wax - scattering (e.g. specular)
v. NIR - Cell morphology (structure of the spongy mesophyll)
v. MIR - Water absorption features

4.2.1 Leaves –reflectance (peak) and absorption (valley) bands

Chlorophyll, for example, strongly absorbs energy in the wavelength bands centred at about 0.45 µm and 0.65 µm. Hence our eyes perceive healthy vegetation as green in colour because of the very high absorption of blue and red energy by plant leaves and the very high reflection of green energy. As we go from the visible to the reflected infrared portion of the spectrum beyond 0.7 µm the reflectance of healthy vegetation increases dramatically. In the range from about 0.7 µm to 1.3 µm, a plant leaf reflects about 50 percent of the energy incident on it. Plant reflectance in the 0.7 to 1.3 µm range results primarily from the internal structure is highly variable between plant species. Reflectance measurement in this range often permits us to discriminate between species, even if they look the same in visible wavelengths. Beyond 1.3 µm, energy incident upon vegetation is essentially absorbed or reflected, with little to no transmittance of energy. Prominent dips in reflectance occur at 1.4 µm, 1.9 µm and 2.7 µm because the water in the leaf absorbs strongly at these wavelengths.

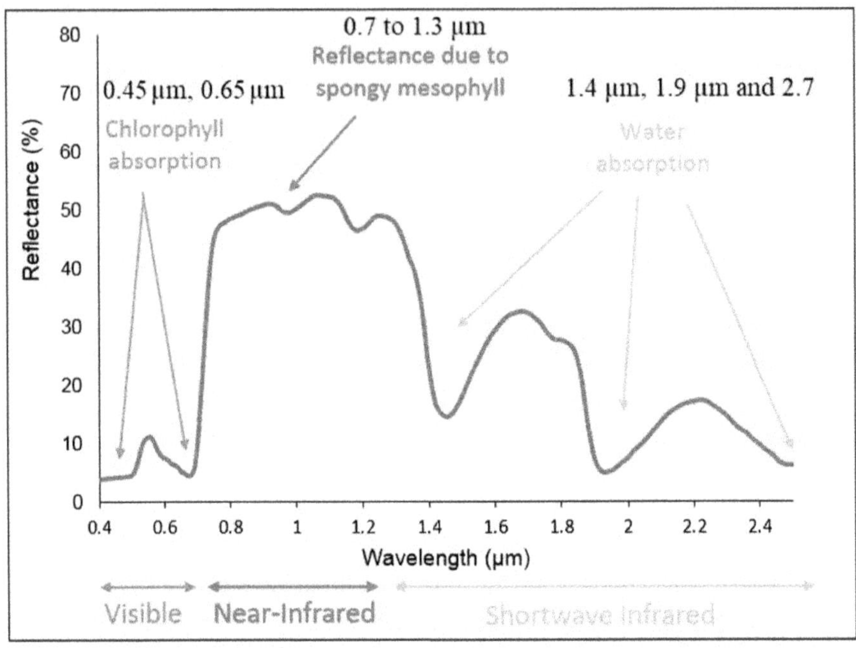

Figure 4.4 Vegetation spectral reflectance curves

NIR reflectance will change with stress:

- Disease
- Water stress
- Old age
- Changes before Visible

NIR reflectance:

- Shows where a problem is occurring
- Does not identify the problem
- Will detect the problem prior to visible inspection
- Will monitor recovery

4.2.2 Factors responsible for the reflection of energy from vegetation

1. Pigment
2. Structural pattern of leaves
3. Water content in the leaves
4. Effect of soil as a background
5. Solar elevation/incident angle
6. Effect of canopy geometry
7. Position of leaves
8. Effect of vegetation senescence
9. Change of pigment
10. Plant suffers from disease (Figure 4.5)

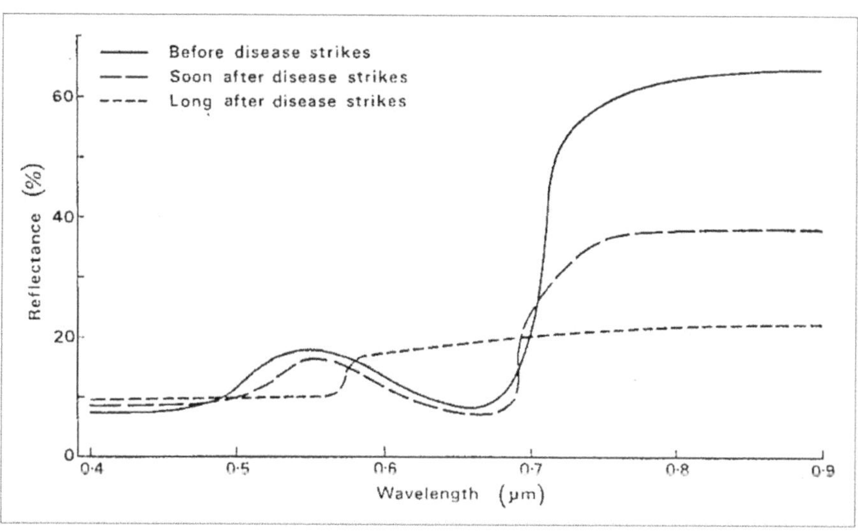

Figure 4.5 Vegetation spectral reflectance curves

4.3 Spatial reflectance curve for Water

Longer wavelength visible and near-infrared radiation is absorbed more by water than shorter visible wavelengths. Thus water typically looks blue or blue-green due to stronger reflectance at these shorter wavelengths, and darker if viewed at red or near-infrared wavelengths (Campbell and Wynne, 2011).

Chlorophyll in algae absorbs more of the blue wavelengths and reflects the green, making the water appear deep green in colour when algae are present (Figure 4.6a). If there are suspended sediment present in the upper layers of the water body, then this will allow better reflectivity and a brighter appearance of the water (Figure 4.6b). The apparent colour of the water will show a slight shift to longer wavelengths. Suspended sediment (S) can be easily confused with shallow (but clear) water since these two phenomena appear very similar. The topography of the water surface (rough, smooth, floating materials, etc.) can also lead to complications for water-related interpretation due to potential problems of specular reflection and other influences on colour and brightness (CCRS, 2009).

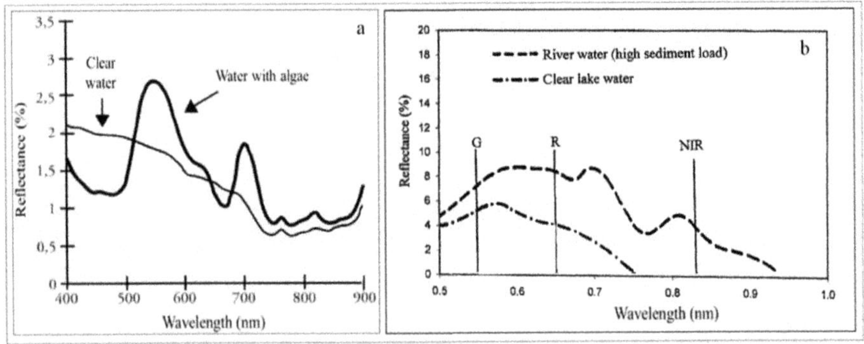

Figure 4.6 Reflectance characteristics from (a) clear water vs. clear water with algae and (b) clear water [lake] vs. turbid [river] water

Factors responsible for the reflection of energy from water

1. Depth of water
2. Materials suspended in the water
3. Surface roughness
4. Incident angle of energy on the water

4.4 Spatial reflectance curve for Soil

The soil curve shows considerably fewer peak and valley variations in reflectance. That is the factors that influence soil reflectance act over less specific spectral bands. Some of the factors affecting soil reflectance are moisture content, soil texture (proportion of sand, silt and clay), surface roughness, the presence of iron oxide and organic matter content. These factors are complex, variable and interrelated. For example, the presence of moisture in the soil will decrease its reflectance (Figure 4.7). Soil moisture content is strongly related to the soil texture: coarse sandy soils are usually well drained resulting in low moisture content and have relatively high reflectance; poorly drained fine-textured soils will generally have lower reflectance. Two other factors that reduce soil reflectance are surface roughness and the content of organic matter. The presence of iron oxide in soil will also significantly decrease reflectance at least in the lower part of visible wavelength (Campbell and Wynne, 2011).

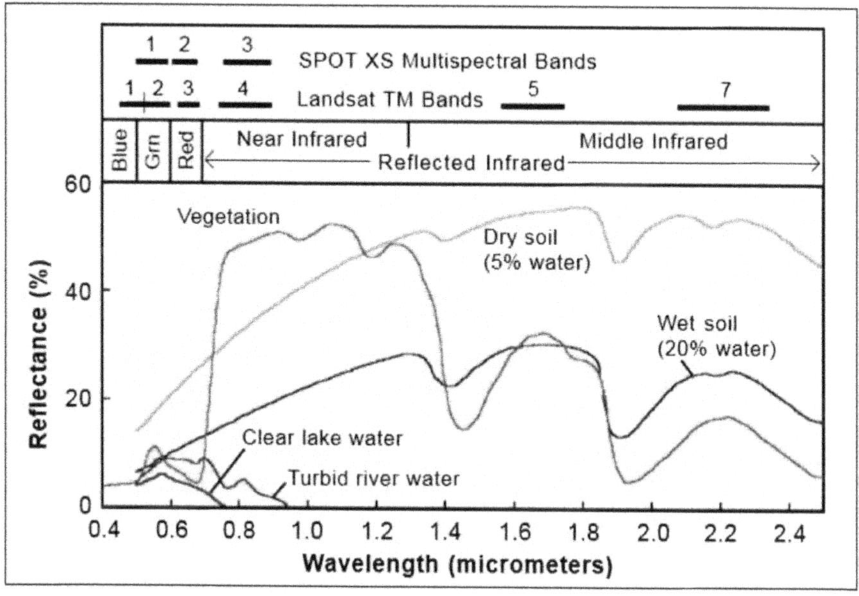

Figure 4.7 Spectral reflectance curve of different types of soil and water

Factors responsible for reflection of energy from soil

1. Moisture contents
2. Organic matter
3. Natural minerals
4. Soil texture
5. Soil compactness/structure
6. Soil colour
7. Gravel or stoniness

4.5 Peak and valley for water, vegetation and dry soil

As previously mentioned here is the summary of the characteristics of reflectance and absorbance of different wavelengths portion by clear water, healthy vegetation and dry soil. The significant reflectance referred to peaks and absorbance referred to valleys (Figure 4.8).

Clear Water

(Peak) 0.6 µm

Green vegetation

(Peak) 0.7 to 1.3 µm; 0.5 µm; 1.6 µm; 2.2 µm;

(Valley): 0.45 µm; 0.65 µm [chlorophyll absorption]; 1.4 µm, 1.9 µm and 2.7 µm [water absorption bands]

Dry Soil

(Peak) 1.6 µm;

(Valley) 0.9 µm; 1.4 µm, 1.9 µm 2.2 µm and 2.7 µm

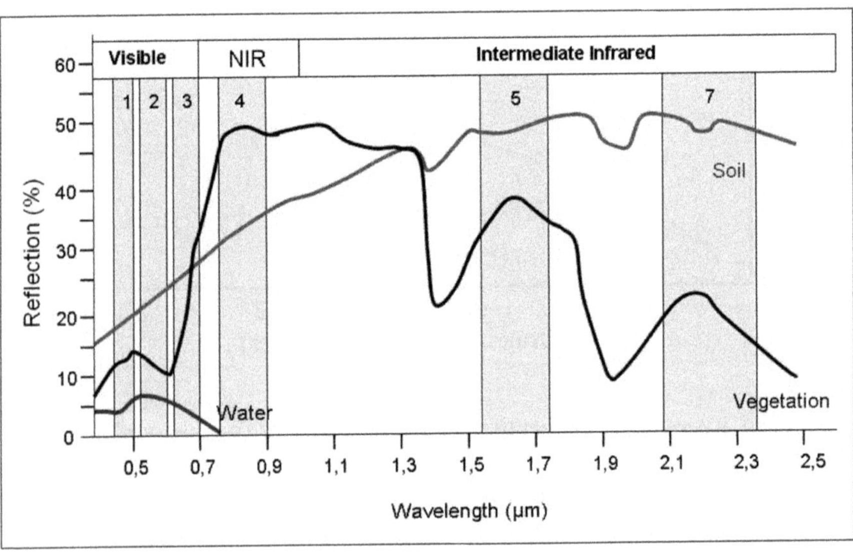

Figure 4.8 Spectral reflectance curves with peaks and valleys of different types of soil and water

4.6 Spectral Signature / Spectral Response Patterns

From the study of the spectral reflectance characteristics of vegetation, soil and water, we should recognise that these broad feature types are normally spectrally separable. However, the degree of separation between types is a function of 'where we look spectrally'. For example, water and vegetation might reflect nearly equally in visible wavelengths. Yet these features are almost always separable in reflective infrared wavelengths. Because spectral responses measured by remote sensors over various features often permit an assessment of the type and/or conditions of the features, these responses have been referred to as spectral signatures (Campbell and Wynne, 2011).

The reflectance of clear water is generally low. However, the reflectance is maximum at the blue end of the spectrum and decreases as the wavelength increases. Hence, clear water appears dark-bluish. Turbid water has some sediment suspension, which increases the reflectance in the red end of the spectrum, accounting for its brownish appearance. The reflectance of bare soil generally depends on its composition. In the example shown, the reflectance increases monotonically with increasing wavelength. Hence, it should appear yellowish-red to the eye.

Vegetation has a unique spectral signature, which enables it to be distinguished readily from other types of land cover in an optical / near-infrared image. The reflectance is low in both the blue and red regions of the spectrum, due to absorption by chlorophyll for photosynthesis. It has a peak in the green region. In the near-infrared (NIR) region, the reflectance is much higher than that in the visible band due to the cellular structure in the leaves. Hence, vegetation can be identified by the high NIR but generally low visible reflectance. This property has been used in early reconnaissance missions during war times for "camouflage detection".

The shape of the reflectance spectrum can be used for the identification of vegetation type. For example, the reflectance spectra of different vegetation species shown in the above illustrations can be distinguished although they exhibit the general characteristic of high NIR but low visible reflectances. One species might have higher reflectance in the visible region but lower reflectance in the NIR region. For the same vegetation type, the reflectance spectrum also depends on other factors such as the leaf moisture content and health of the plants. These properties enable vegetation conditions to be monitored using satellite remote sensing images.

CHAPTER FIVE

Resolution of a Sensor, Sensor Type, Scanning System, and Data Rate

Learning Outcomes

On completion of this chapter students will be able to:

1. Understand the concept of resolution of a remote sensing sensor
2. Explain various types of remote sensing
3. Identify types of satellite images collected through the remote sensing process
4. Illustrate types of the scanning systems of different remote sensing sensors
5. Assess different applications of remote sensing

5.1 Resolution of a sensor

Resolution refers to the intensity or rate of sampling, and extent refers to the overall coverage of a data set. An extent can be seen as relating to the largest feature, or range of features, which can be observed, while resolution relates to the smallest. For a feature to be distinguishable in the data, the resolution and extent of the measurement dimensions of the data set need to be appropriate to the measurable properties of the feature. For a feature to be separable from other features, these measurements must also be able to discriminate between the differences in reflectance from the features

(Lillesand et al., 2015).

Resolution and extent can be seen to operate in four 'dimensions' of remotely sensed data acquisition:

1. **Spatial**: resolution relates to pixel size, the extent to the overall image coverage
2. **Spectral**: resolution relates to the width of wavelength channels, extent describes the number and spectral range of channels in the image
3. **Radiometric**: resolution relates to the energy difference which determines different radiation (or brightness) levels in an image, extent to the number of levels detected
4. **Temporal**: resolution relates to the repeat cycle or interval between successive acquisitions, the extent to the total period over which imagery is available.

5.1.1 Spatial resolution

Spatial resolution defines the level of spatial detail depicted in an image. This may be described as a measure of the smallness of objects on the ground that may be distinguished as separate entities in the image, with the smallest object necessarily being larger than a single pixel. In this sense, spatial resolution is directly related to image pixel size (Figure 5.1). In terms of photographic data, an image pixel may be compared to grain size while spatial resolution is more closely related to photographic scale.

The pixel size for satellite-borne scanners is a function of the sensor (optics and sampling rate) and the platform (altitude and velocity). Landsat ETM+ has a nominal pixel size of 30 x 30 m. SPOT, have smaller pixels (10/ 20 m) giving fine detail for specific features, but generating too much data to be used conveniently for large area studies.

Measurements in remotely sensed imagery are usually obtained by sampling the Earth's surface using a constant view angle. This angle is referred to as the Instantaneous Field of View (IFOV) and determines the ground area 'viewed' to form a pixel or the 'optical' pixel size. So the pixel size is depending upon two factors, IFOV, and the Height of the sensor. If the IFOV become more so the spatial coverage will be big and vice versa. Also if the height of the sensor becomes more so the spatial coverage will be big and vice versa.

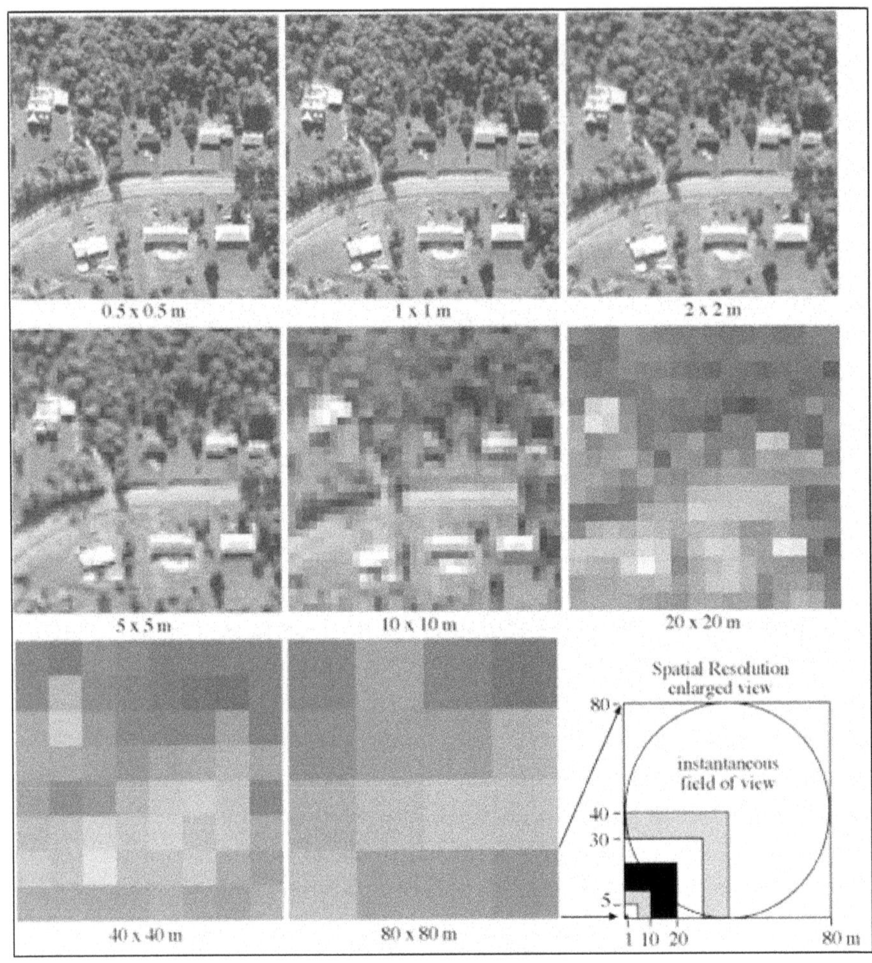

Figure 5.1 Variation of spatial resolution of a sensor

<u>**PROBLEM:**</u> SUPPOSE THE HEIGHT OF A SENSOR IS 900Km AND THE IFOV IS 40 µradian, SO WHAT WILL BE THE SPATIAL RESOLUTION OF THE SENSOR?

<u>**SOLVE:**</u> SPATIAL RESOLUTION=HEIGHT x IFOV = 900Km x 40 µradian

=900000m x 40/1000000radian

=36m

A **"High Resolution"** image refers to one with a small resolution size. Fine details can be seen in a high-resolution image. On the other hand, a **"Low Resolution"** image is one with a large resolution size, i.e. only coarse features can be observed in the image.

5.1.2 Spectral resolution

The spectral resolution is related to the width of EMR used by the detector to collect the information about earth's surface phenomena. Different classes of features and details in an image can often be distinguished by comparing their responses over distinct wavelength ranges. Broad classes, such as water and vegetation, can usually be separated using very broad wavelength ranges - the visible and near-infrared. Other more specific classes, such as different rock types, may not be easily distinguishable using either of these broad wavelength ranges and would require comparison at much finer wavelength ranges to separate them. Thus, we would require a sensor with higher **spectral resolution.** Spectral resolution describes the ability of a sensor to define fine wavelength intervals. The finer the spectral resolution, the narrower the wavelength ranges for a particular channel or band (Campbell and Wynne, 2011). Black and white film records wavelengths extending over much, or the entire visible portion of the electromagnetic spectrum (Figure 5.2). Its spectral resolution is fairly coarse, as the various wavelengths of the visible spectrum are not individually distinguished and the overall reflectance in the entire visible portion is recorded. Color film is also sensitive to the reflected energy over the visible portion of the spectrum, but has a higher spectral resolution, as it is individually sensitive to the reflected energy at the blue, green, and red wavelengths of the spectrum (Figure 5.2). Thus, it can represent features of various colors based on their reflectance in each of these distinct wavelength ranges.

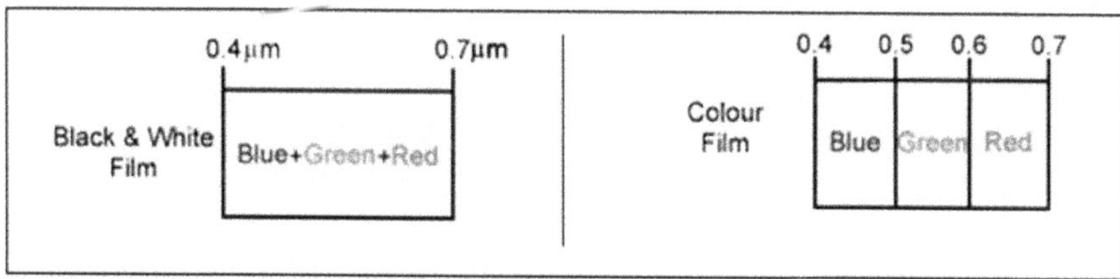

Figure 5.2 Spectral characteristics of a black & white film and colour film

Many remote sensing systems record energy over several separate wavelengths ranges at various spectral resolutions. These are referred to as **multi-spectral sensors** (Figure 5.3). Advanced multi-spectral sensors called **hyper-spectral** sensors, detect hundreds of very narrow spectral bands throughout the visible, near-infrared, and mid-infrared portions of the electromagnetic spectrum. Their very high spectral resolution facilitates fine discrimination between different targets based on their spectral response in each of the narrow bands.

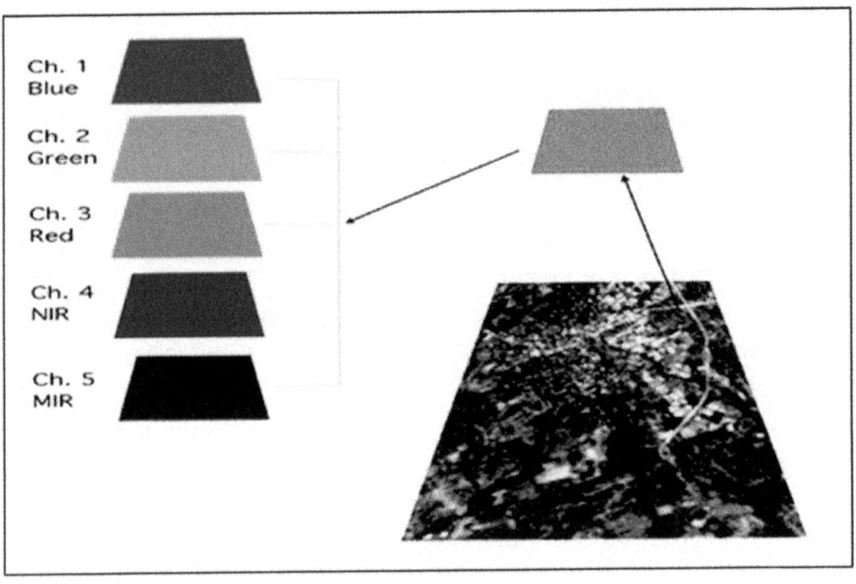

Figure 5.3 Multispectral imagery: the layers of a Landsat Image

5.1.3 Radiometric resolution

Radiometric resolution is related to the number of discrete grey levels recorded by the detector. **Radiometric Resolution** refers to the smallest change in intensity level that can be detected by the sensing system. The radiometric resolution of a sensing system depends on the signal-to-noise ratio of the detector. In a digital image, the radiometric resolution is limited by the number of discrete quantization levels used to digitize the continuous intensity value. Most remotely sensed imagery is recorded with quantization levels in the range 0 & 255, that is, the minimum 'detectable' radiation level is recorded as 0 while the 'maximum' radiation is recorded as 255. This range is also referred to as 8-bit resolution since all values in the range may be represented by 8 bits (binary digits) in a computer (Figure

5.4). Quantization levels are frequently given in terms of the number of bits rather than the number or range of levels (Lillesand et al., 2015). These values are related by:

$$2^{\text{number of bits}} = \text{number of quantisation levels}$$

Number of bits	Number of quantisation levels	Range of quantisation levels
1	2	0-1
2	4	0-3
3	8	0-7
4	16	0-15
5	32	0-31
6	64	0-63
7	128	0-127
8	256	0-255
9	512	0-511
10	1024	0-1023

Figure 5.4 Grey levels based on computer binary digits

In image processing, quantization levels are usually referred to as Digital Numbers (DN). The finer the radiometric resolution of a sensor, the more sensitive it is to detect small differences in reflected or emitted energy. A couple of images shown below evince the impact of radiometric resolution on the picture contrast (Figure 5.5).

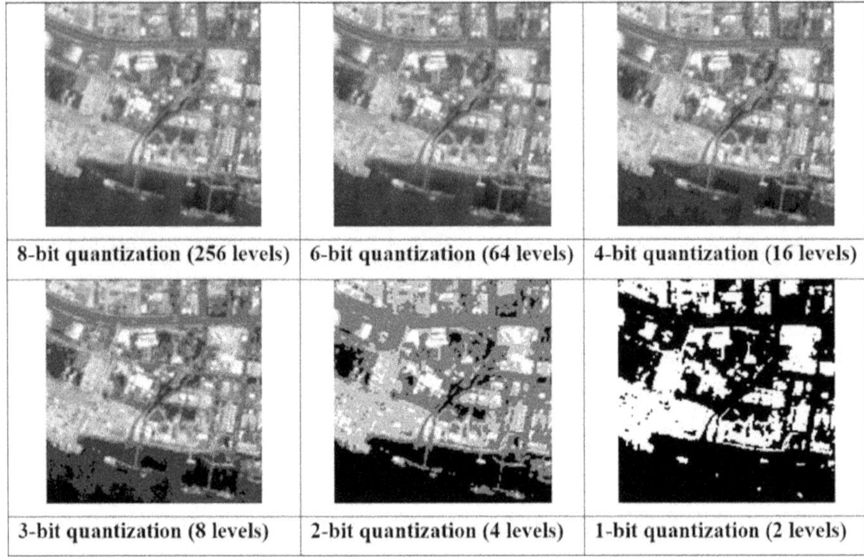

Figure 5.5 Example different radiometric satellite data

5.1.4 Temporal Resolution

The temporal resolution of remotely sensed data refers to the repeat cycle or interval between acquisitions of successive imagery. This cycle is fixed for spacecraft platforms by their orbital characteristics. The concept of revisit period refers to the length of time it takes for a satellite to complete one entire orbit cycle. The revisit period of a satellite sensor is usually several days. Therefore the absolute temporal resolution of a remote sensing system to image the exact same area at the same viewing angle a second time is equal to this period. However, because of some degree of overlap in the imaging swaths of adjacent orbits for most satellites and the increase in this overlap with increasing latitude, some areas of the Earth tend to be re-imaged more frequently. Also, some satellite systems are able to point their sensors to image the same area between different satellite passes separated by periods from one to five days. Thus, the actual temporal resolution of a sensor depends on a variety of factors, including the satellite/sensor capabilities, the swath overlap, and latitude (Figure 5.6). The ability to collect imagery of the same area of the Earth's surface at different periods of time is one of the most important elements for applying remote sensing data. Spectral characteristics of features may change over time and these changes can be detected by collecting and comparing **multi-temporal** imagery (Campbell and Wynne, 2011).

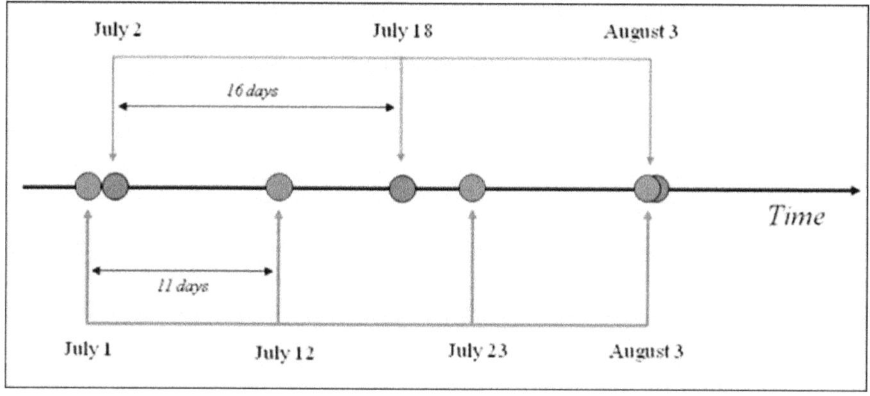

Figure 5.6 Concept of temporal resolution

For example, during the growing season, most species of vegetation are in a continual state of change and our ability to monitor those subtle changes using remote sensing is dependent on when and how frequently we collect imagery. Temporal resolution can be varied from sensor to sensor. For example-

- IRS IA/IB path is 22 days.
- IRS IA/IB path is 24 days.
- LANDSAT- 1, 2, 3 path is 18days.

5.2 Types of Remote Sensing

Remote Sensing can be divided into the following various categories with respect to wavelength regions, photographic systems, and energy resources (Lillesand et al., 2015).

i. Various types of Remote Sensing with respect to Wavelength Regions

- Visible and Reflective Infrared Remote Sensing
- Thermal Infrared Remote Sensing
- Microwave Remote Sensing

ii. Types of sensor According to the photographic system:

- **Imaging Sensor:** This type of sensor generates pictorial output according to the response of Objects. The digital Numbers against pixels are converted into gray/tonal form.

  Example: Landsat-7, ETM+; IRS-LISS III, etc.

- **Non-imaging Sensor:** This type of sensor generates numeric output according to the response of Objects. Example: Specto radiometer; non-imaging radiometer.

iii. The various types of Remote Sensing available with respect to Energy Resources

- **Passive Remote Sensing:** Makes use of sensors that detect the reflected or emitted electromagnetic radiation from natural sources.
- **Active Remote Sensing:** Makes use of sensors that detect reflected responses from objects that are irradiated from artificially generated energy sources, such as Radar/Lidar.

Passive vs. Active Sensing

The sun provides a very convenient source of energy for remote sensing. The sun's energy is either **reflected**, as it is for visible wavelengths, or absorbed and then **re-emitted**, as it is for thermal infrared wavelengths. Remote sensing systems which measure the energy that is naturally available are called passive sensors (Figure 5.7). Passive sensors can only be used to detect energy when naturally occurring energy is available (Lillesand et al., 2015). For all reflected energy, this can only take place during the time when the sun is illuminating the Earth. There is no reflected energy available from the sun at night. The energy that is naturally emitted (such as thermal infrared) can be detected day or night, as long as the amount of energy is large enough to be recorded (CCRS, 2009).

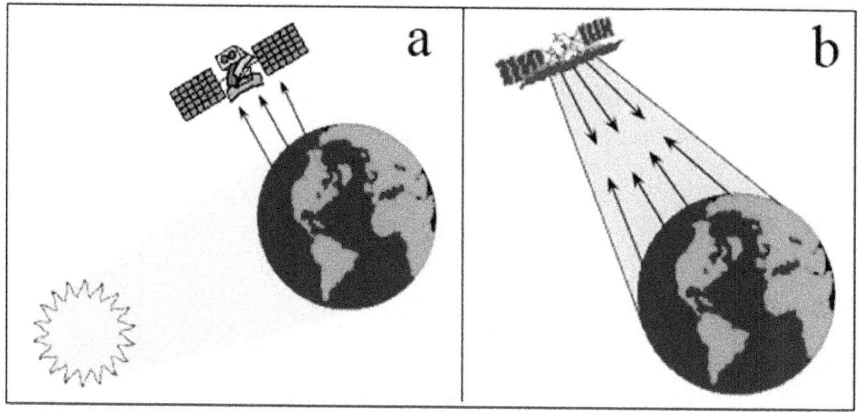

Figure 5.7 (a) Passive vs. (b) active remote sensing

Active sensors, on the other hand, provide their own energy source for illumination. The sensor emits radiation which is directed toward the target to be investigated. The radiation reflected from that target is detected and measured by the sensor (Figure 5.7). Active sensors' advantages include obtaining measurements anytime, regardless of the time of day or season. Active sensors can be used for examining wavelengths that are not sufficiently provided by the sun, such as microwaves, or to better control the way a target is illuminated. However, active systems require the generation of a fairly large amount of energy to adequately illuminate targets. Some examples of active sensors are a laser sensor and synthetic aperture radar (SAR) (CCRS, 2009).

5.3 Types of Satellite image

5.3.1 Panchromatic Images

A panchromatic image consists of only one band. It is usually displayed as a grey scale image, i.e. the displayed brightness of a particular pixel is proportional to the pixel digital number which is related to the intensity of solar radiation reflected by the targets in the pixel and detected by the detector. Thus, a panchromatic image may be similarly interpreted as a black-and-white aerial photograph of the area, though at a lower resolution. The picture (Figure 5.8) shows a panchromatic image extracted from a SPOT panchromatic scene at a ground resolution of 10 m. The ground coverage is about 6.5 km (width) by 5.5 km (height). The urban area at the bottom left and a clearing near the top of the image have high reflected intensity, while the vegetated areas on the right part of the image are generally dark. Roads and blocks of buildings in the urban area are visible. A river flowing through the vegetated area, cutting across the top right corner of the image can be seen. The river appears bright due to sediments while the sea at the bottom edge of the image appears dark (Lillesand et al., 2015).

Figure 5.8 Panchromatic satellite image

5.3.2 Multispectral Images

A multispectral image consists of several bands of data. For visual display, each band of the image may be displayed one band at a time as a greyscale image, or in a combination of three bands at a time as a colour composite image. Interpretation of a multispectral colour composite image will require knowledge of the spectral reflectance signature of the targets in the scene. Figure 5.9 shows the three bands of a multispectral image extracted from a SPOT multispectral scene at a ground resolution of 20 m (Lillesand et al., 2015). The area covered is the same as that shown in the above panchromatic image. Note that both the XS1 (green) and

XS2 (red) bands look almost identical to the panchromatic image shown above. In contrast, the vegetated areas now appear bright in the XS3 (near infrared) band due to the high reflectance of leaves in the near-infrared wavelength region. Several shades of grey can be identified for vegetated areas, corresponding to different types of vegetation. Water mass (both the river and the sea) appear dark in the XS3 (near IR) band (Campbell and Wynne, 2011).

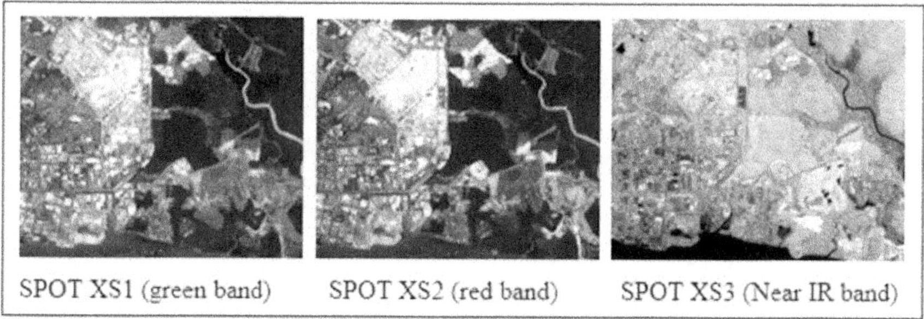

Figure 5.9 Multi-spectral bands of SPOT satellite image

5.4 Satellite data color composition

5.4.1 Standard false colour composite (SFCC)

The display colour assignment for any band of a multispectral image can be done in an entirely arbitrary manner. In this case, the colour of a target in the displayed image does not have any resemblance to its actual colour. The resulting product is known as a false colour composite (FCC) image. There are many possible schemes for producing false colour composite images. However, some schemes may be more suitable for detecting certain objects in the image (Campbell and Wynne, 2011).

A very common false color composite scheme for displaying a SPOT multispectral image is shown below:

R = XS3 (NIR band)

G = XS2 (red band)

B = XS1 (green band)

This standard false color composite scheme allows vegetation to be detected readily in the image. In this type of false-color composite image, vegetation appears in different shades of red depending on the types and conditions of the vegetation, since it has a high reflectance in the NIR band. Clearwater appears dark-bluish (higher green band reflectance), while turbid water appears cyan (higher red reflectance due to sediments) compared to clear water. Bare soils, roads, and buildings may appear in various shades of blue, yellow, or grey, depending on their composition as figure 5.10.

Figure 5.10 False colour composite of a SPOT image

5.4.2 Natural Color Composite

When displaying a natural color composite image, the spectral bands (some of which may not be in the visible region) are combined in such a way that the appearance of the displayed image resembles a visible color photograph, i.e. vegetation in green, water in blue, soil in brown or grey, etc. Many people refer to this composite as a "true color" composite. However, this term may be misleading since in many instances the colors are only simulated to look similar to the "true" colors of the targets.

For example, the bands 3 (red band), 2 (green band), and 1 (blue band) of a LANDSAT TM image can be assigned respectively to the R, G, and B colour for display. In this way, the colors of the resulting color composite image resemble closely what would be observed by the human eyes. The SPOT HRV multispectral sensor does not have a blue band. The three bands, XS1, XS2, and XS3 correspond to the green, red, and NIR bands respectively. But a reasonably good natural color composite can be produced by the following combination (Lillesand et al., 2015) of the spectral bands (Figure 5.11):

R = XS2

G = (3 XS1 + XS3)/4

B = (3 XS1 - XS3)/4

Figure 5.11 Natural color composite of a multispectral SPOT image

5.5 Scanning system and its type

Many electronic (as opposed to photographic) remote sensors acquire data using scanning systems, which employ a sensor with a narrow field of view (i.e. IFOV) that sweeps over the terrain to build up and produce a two-dimensional image of the surface. Scanning systems can be used on both aircraft and satellite platforms and have essentially the same operating principles (Lillesand et al., 2015). A scanning system used to collect data over a variety of different wavelength ranges is called a multispectral scanner (MSS), and is the most commonly used scanning system. There are two main modes or methods of scanning employed to acquire multispectral image data - across-track scanning, and along-track scanning (CCRS, 2009).

5.5.1 Across-track scanning

Across-track scanners (Figure 5.12) scan the Earth in a series of lines. The lines are oriented perpendicular to the direction of motion of the sensor platform (i.e. across the swath). Each line is scanned from one side of the sensor to the other, using a rotating mirror (A). As the platform moves forward over the Earth, successive scans build up a two-dimensional image of the Earth's surface (Lillesand et al., 2015). The incoming reflected or emitted radiation is separated into several spectral components detected independently. The UV, visible, near-infrared, and thermal radiation are dispersed into their constituent wavelengths. A bank of internal detectors (B), each sensitive to a specific range of wavelengths, detects and measures the energy for each spectral band, and then, as an electrical signal, they are converted to digital data and recorded for subsequent computer processing. Across-track scanners scan the Earth in a series of lines. The IFOV (C) of the sensor and the altitude of the platform determines the ground resolution cell viewed (D), and thus the spatial resolution. The angular field of view (E) is the sweep of the mirror, measured in degrees, used to record a scan line, and determines the width of the imaged swath (F) (CCRS, 2009).

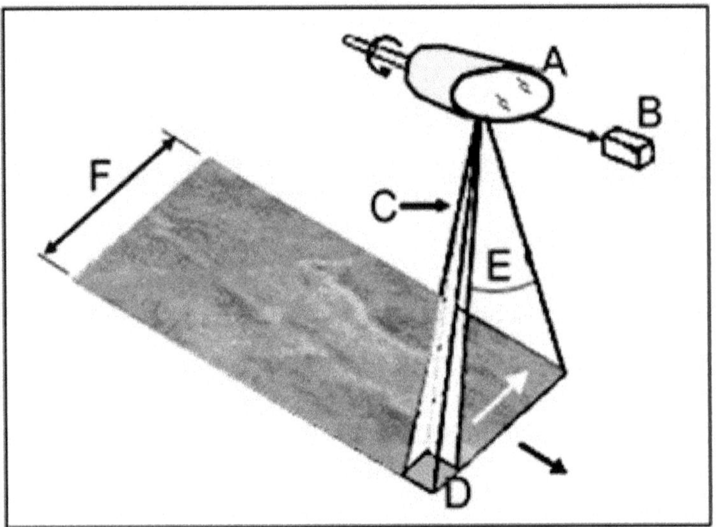

Figure 5.12 Across-track scanning system

5.5.2 Along-track scanning

Along-track scanners (Figure 5.13) also use the forward motion of the platform to record successive scan lines and build up a two-dimensional image, perpendicular to the flight direction. However, instead of a scanning mirror, they use a linear array of detectors (A) located at the focal plane of the image (B) formed by lens systems (C), which are "pushed" along in the flight track direction (i.e. along-track). These systems are also referred to as push broom scanners, as the motion of the detector array is analogous to the bristles of a broom being pushed along a floor. Each individual detector measures the energy for a single ground resolution cell (D) and thus the size and IFOV of the detectors determine the spatial resolution of the system. A separate linear array is required to measure each spectral band or channel. For each scan line, the energy detected by each detector of each linear array is sampled electronically and digitally recorded (CCRS, 2009).

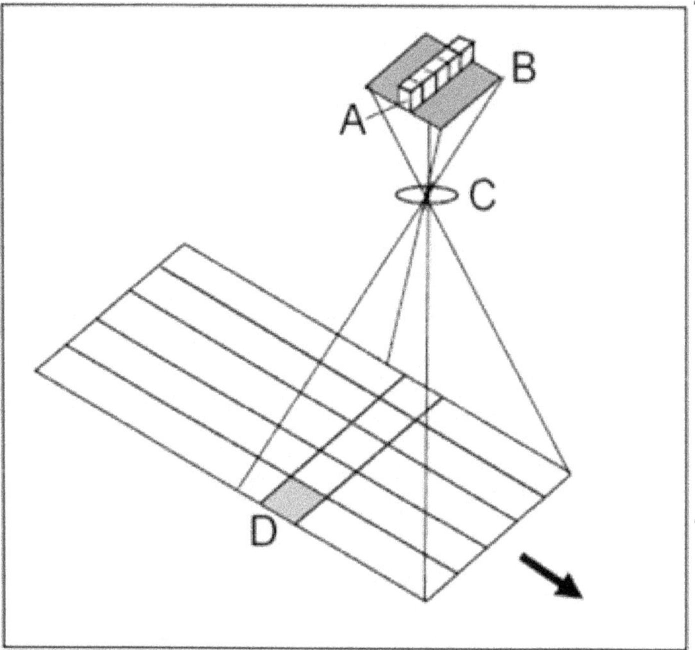

Figure 5.13 Across-track scanning system

5.6 Sensor's data rate

The data rate is the volume of data collected during the scanning process by a satellite sensor within a specified unit of time. The units used for this are baud or bits/s. Demand for better resolution images from remote sensing satellites is increasing the amount of data to be transmitted in real-time compared to the low spatial resolution data. To calculate a sensor's data rate following equation (Table 5.1) can be used:

(No of Line x No of Pixel x No of Band x Radiometric Resolution)/20sec

Table 5.1 Parameters for the calculation of data rate of Landsat-8, OLI sensor

Bands	Spatial Resolution (m)	Radiometric Resolution (bit)	Swath (km)	
B1	30	12 bit	185	185
B2	30		185	185
B3	30		185	185
B4	30		185	185
B5	30		185	185
B6	30		185	185
B7	30		185	185
B9	30		185	185
B8	15		185	185
B10	100		185	185
B11	100		185	185

Equation:

[No of line x No of Pixel x No of Band x Radiometric Resolution] / [Time to scan one scene]

Where, SR: Spatial resolution

Swath: The length/width of the satellite image (one scene)

No. of Lines: (Swath/spatial resolution)

No. of pixel: (Swath/spatial resolution)

RR: Radiometric resolution

The approximate time to scan one scene is considered 20 sec

Unit conversion: 1048576 bit = 1 Megabit

Table 2 Calculated data rate of Landsat-8, OLI sensor

	S R (m)	Swath (km)		Line (Swath/SR)	Pixel (Swath/SR)	RR	Approximate Time to scan one scene	Data Rate	TOTAL
B1	30	185	185	6167	6167	12 Bit	20 sec	21.76	174.10
B2	30	185	185	6167	6167			21.76	
B3	30	185	185	6167	6167			21.76	
B4	30	185	185	6167	6167			21.76	
B5	30	185	185	6167	6167			21.76	
B6	30	185	185	6167	6167			21.76	
B7	30	185	185	6167	6167			21.76	
B9	30	185	185	6167	6167			21.76	
B8	15	185	185	12333	12333			87.03	87.03
B10	100	185	185	1850	1850			1.96	3.92
B11	100	185	185	1850	1850			1.96	
Total Data rate								265.05MB/SEC	

5.7 Applications of Satellite Imagery & Remote Sensing Data

Remote sensing data provide essential information that helps in monitoring various applications such as image fusion, change detection, and land cover classification. Remote sensing is a key technique used to obtain information related to the earth's resources and environment. What popularized satellite imagery data, is that they can be easily accessed online through various mapping applications like Google Earth and Bing Maps. From being simply able to find, "where is my house" these applications have helped the GIS community in project planning, monitoring disasters and natural calamities, and guiding civil defense people.

Remotely sensed satellite images and data include spectral, spatial, and temporal resolutions. Spectral statistics involves elements of remotely sensed image classification. The main aspect which influences the accuracy of the ground objects is spatial resolution. Temporal resolution helps in the generation of land cover maps for environmental planning, land use change detection, and transportation planning. Data integration and analysis of urban areas using medium resolution remote sensing imagery mainly focuses on the documentation of built-up areas or is used for differentiating between residential, commercial, and industrial zones.

- ***Providing a base map for graphical reference and assisting planners and engineers***

The amount of detail that ortho-imagery produces using high-resolution satellite imagery is of immense value as it provides a detailed image of the selected area along with its surrounding areas.

Maps are location-based they are specifically designed to communicate highly structured data and to give a complete picture of the whole world. There are numerous applications of satellite imagery and remote sensing data. Today nations use information derived from satellite imagery for government decision-making, civil defense operations, police, and Geographic Information Systems (GIS) in general. These days, data captured through Satellite Imagery has become mandatory and all government plans are to be submitted on the basis of Satellite Imagery data.

- ***Extracting mineral deposits with remote sensing based spectral analysis***

During the pre-feasibility and feasibility stages of the mineral exploration, it is important to know about the mineral potentiality of the area to be considered for mineral extraction. In such scenarios, satellite remote sensing-based mapping and its integration into a GIS platform help geoscientists map the mineral potential zones easily by saving time. With the help of spectral analysis of satellite image bands, scientists can quickly identify and map mineral availability through special indicators. This will enable exploration geologists to narrow his geophysical, geochemical and test drilling activities to high potential zones.

- ***Disaster mitigation planning and recovery***

The result of a natural calamity can be devastating and at times difficult to assess. But disaster risk assessment is necessary for rescue workers. This information has to be prepared and executed quickly and with accuracy. Object-based image classification using change detection (pre- and post-event) is a quick way to acquire damage assessment data. Other similar applications using satellite imagery in disaster assessments include measuring shadows from buildings and digital surface models.

- ***Agriculture Development***

With the increasing population across the world and the need for increased agricultural production, there is a certain need for proper management of the world's agricultural resources. To make this happen it is first necessary to obtain reliable data on not only the types but also the quality, quantity, and location of these resources. Satellite imagery and GIS (Geographic Information Systems) will always continue to be significant factor in the improvement of the present systems of acquiring and generating agricultural maps and resource data. Agriculture mapping and surveys are presently conducted throughout the world, in order to gather information and statistics on crops, range land, livestock, and other related agricultural resources.

This information collected is necessary for the implementation of effective management decisions. The agricultural survey is needed for planning and allocation of the limited resources to different sectors of the economy.

- *3D GIS*

3D city models are digital models of urban areas that represent Terrain surfaces, sites, buildings, vegetation, infrastructure, and Landscape elements as well as related objects belonging to urban areas. Their components are described and represented by corresponding two-dimensional and three-dimensional spatial data and geo-referenced data. 3D city models support the presentation, exploration, analysis, and management of tasks in a large number of different application domains. 3D GIS is the instant and effective solution for larger and remote locations where the manual survey is next to impossible. Various urban/ rural planning departments require 3D GIS data like Drainage, Sewerage, water supply, Canal Designing BIM, and many more.

5.8 Applications of communication satellites

Satellites that are launched into orbit by using rockets are called man-made satellites or artificial satellites. Artificial satellites revolve around the earth because of the gravitational force of attraction between the earth and satellites. Unlike natural satellites (moon), artificial satellites are used in various applications. The various applications of artificial satellites include:

- ***Weather forecasting***

Weather forecasting is the prediction of the future of weather. The satellites that are used to predict the future of weather are called weather satellites. Weather satellites continuously monitor the climate and weather conditions of the earth. They use sensors called radiometers for measuring the heat energy released from the earth's surface. Weather satellites also predict the most dangerous storms such as hurricanes.

- ***Navigation***

Generally, navigation refers to determining the geographical location of an object. The satellites that are used to determine the geographic location of aircraft, ships, cars, trains, or any other object are called navigation satellites. GPS (Global Positioning System) is an example of a navigation system. It allows the user to determine their exact location anywhere in the world.

- ***Astronomy***

Astronomy is the study of celestial objects such as stars, planets, galaxies, natural satellites, comets, etc. The satellites that are used to study or observe the distant stars, galaxies, planets, etc. are called astronomical satellites. They are mainly used to find the new stars, planets, and galaxies. Hubble space telescope is an example of astronomical satellite. It captures the high-resolution images of the distant stars, galaxies, planets etc.

- ***Satellite phone***

A satellite phone is a type of mobile phone that uses satellites instead of cell towers for transmitting signals or information over long distances.

Mobile phones that use cell towers will work only within the coverage area of a cell tower. If we go beyond the coverage area of a cell tower or if we reach remote areas, it becomes difficult to make a voice call or send text messages with mobile phones. Unlike mobile mobiles, satellite phones have global coverage. Satellite phones use geostationary satellites and low earth orbit (LEO) satellites for transmitting information.

When a person makes a call from a satellite phone, the signal is sent to the satellite. The satellite will receive that signal, processes it, and redirects the signal back to the earth via a gateway. The gateway then sends the signal or call to the destination by using the regular cellular and landline networks. The usage of satellite phones is illegal in some countries like Cuba, North Korea, Burma, India, and Russia.

- ***Satellite television***

A satellite television or satellite TV is a wireless system that uses communication satellites to deliver television programs or television signals to the users or viewers.

TV or television mostly uses geostationary satellites because they look stationary from the earth. Hence, the signal is easily transmitted. When the television signal is sent to the satellite, it receives the signal, amplifies it, and retransmits it back to the earth. The first satellite television signal was sent from Europe to North America by using the Telstar satellite.

- *Military satellite*

A military satellite is an artificial satellite used by the army for various purposes such as spying on enemy countries, military communication, and navigation.

Military satellites obtain secret information from enemy countries. These satellites also detect the missiles launched by other countries in space.

- * *Satellite internet*

The satellite internet is a wireless system that uses satellites to deliver internet signals to users. High-speed internet is the main advantage of satellite internet. Satellite internet does not use cable systems, but instead, it uses satellites to transmit the information or signal.

- * *Satellite Radio*

Satellite radio is a wireless transmission service that uses orbiting satellites to deliver information or radio signals to consumers. It is primarily used in cars. When the ground station transmits a signal to the satellite that is revolving around the earth, the satellite receives the signal, amplifies it, and redirects the signal back to the earth (radio receivers in the cars).

CHAPTER SIX

Components of Geographic Information Systems

Learning Outcomes

On completion of this chapter students will be able to:

1. Understand the basics of geographic information system
2. Describe the different segments in the geographic information system

6.1 Definition of GIS

Indeed the most difficult task is to define what GIS conveys that will convince the users of all hues mentioned in the overlying Para. Like the field of geography, the term Geographic Information System (GIS) is hard to define. It represents the integration of many subject areas. Accordingly, there is no absolutely agreed-upon definition of a GIS (DeMers, 1997). A broadly accepted definition of GIS is the one provided by the National Centre of Geographic Information and Analysis (Goodchild, 2002):

"A GIS is a system of hardware, software and procedures to facilitate the management, manipulation, analysis, modelling, representation and display of geo-referenced data to solve complex problems regarding planning and management of resources".

Although wide divergence of view exists with regard to what constitutes a GIS, perhaps the most accepted definition of GIS states:

GIS is a decision support system comprising of computer hardware, software, geographic data, and personnel designed to efficiently capture, store, manipulate, analyse and display all forms of spatial and non-spatial (attribute) data for better management of the geographical area.

An Alternative Definition of GIS: *A GIS is "an organised collection of computer hardware, software, geographic data, and personnel designed to efficiently capture, store, update, manipulate, analyse, and display all forms of geographically referenced information."*

One reason why it is difficult to agree on a single definition for GIS is that various kinds of GIS exist, each made for different purposes and for different types of decision-making.

The Generic Definition of GIS:

Geographic = spatially referenced data

Information = data processed into a usable form for human consumption

System = a framework for manipulating, querying, analysing and disseminating information

A more comprehensive and easy way to define GIS is the one that looks at the disposition, in layers (Figure 6.1), of its data sets. "Group of maps of the same portion of the territory, where a given location has the same coordinates in all the maps included in the system". This way, it is possible to analyse its thematic and spatial characteristics to obtain a better knowledge of this zone.

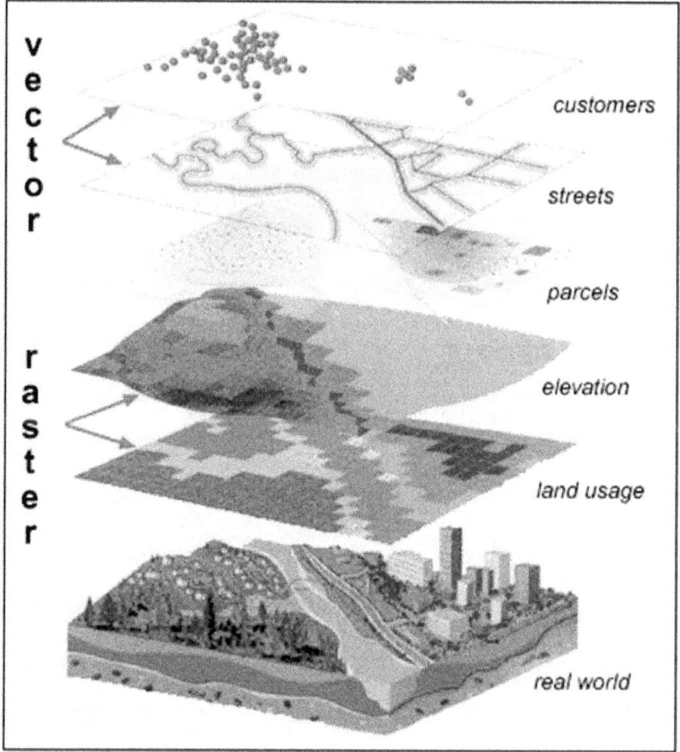

Figure 6.1 The concept of layers (ESRI)

6.2 Components of GIS

A Geographic Information System links locational (Spatial) and database (tabular) information and enables a person to visualize patterns, relationships, and trends. This process gives an entirely new perspective to data analysis that cannot be seen in a table or list format. The five key components of a GIS are listed below (Figure 6.2):

Hardware: Computer and peripherals on which the GIS operates
Methods: Well-designed guidelines, specifications, standards and procedures
People: Users of GIS, technical specialists planners who use GIS
Data: Spatial data, Attribute data, Image data
Software: The functions and tools

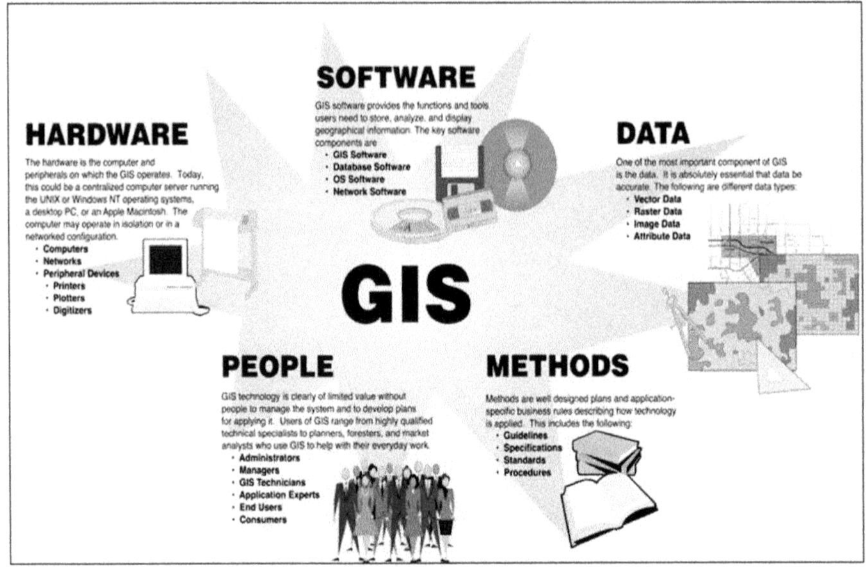

Figure 6.2 Five key components of a GIS

6.2.1 Computer Hardware

The general hardware components of a geographical information system are:

i. The main computer system or the central processing unit (CPU) and
v. The peripherals namely,

- The terminal – keyboard and visual display unit (VDU),
- Digitisers/scanners,
- Disk drive,
- Tape drive,
- Plotter,
- Printer etc.

The main computing unit is the CPU. This is linked to a disk drive, the storage unit. The user interacts with the CPU with the help of a keyboard, via a terminal. Apart from the system hard disk, tape/cartridge/optical disk drives are provided for input/output and storage of data or software. Digitisers or scanners are used to convert the information on maps into digital form to be stored in the computer system for further analysis. A plotter or camera attachment, printer etc. forms the output devices that are used for retrieving the results of the analysis in different forms (plots, tables, photos etc.).

6.2.2 Software Modules

The software package for a GIS consists of five basic technical modules, namely:

1. *Data input, editing and verification*
2. *Data storage and database management*
3. *Data analysis, modelling and cartographic manipulation*
4. *Data output and presentation*
5. *User interface / interaction*

1. Data input, editing and verification: Data for input are acquired in a variety of formats including graphic, descriptive (non-spatial information or attribute) and digital imagery (satellite data) or aerial photographs. Prior to encoding all these data we require manual or automated pre-processing such as, format conversion, error detection and editing, edge matching and registration. Data input covers all aspects of data transformation necessary to form what are called GIS layers.

2. Data storage and database management: Data storage and database management are concerned with the way the data are structured and organised, both with respect to the way they should be handled in the computer and also as prescribed by the users. Data management allows a database to be used through a combination of hardware and software facilities and operations. It is designed to provide i. Effective data storage, retrieval and updating facilities, ii. Multi-user environment, iii. Data independence, security and integrity

***3. Data analysis, modelling and cartographic manipulation*:** One of the most important characteristics of GIS is the capability for data analysis and spatial modelling. Conventional GIS analysis and manipulation capabilities include map overlaying, reclassification procedures, proximity analysis, buffering & corridor techniques, network analysis and other cartographic modelling tools, computed as a function of independent values associated with that location on two or more existing maps.

4. Data output and presentation: Data output and presentation concerns the way the data has to be displayed and the results of the analyses reported to the users. The data may be presented in a variety of ways, such as maps, tables, and figures (graphs and charts). But most users of GIS seem to favour the output that is similar to a conventional map.

5. User interface/interaction: All geographical information systems are made up of complex programs that are capable of many different kinds of operations. It is very cumbersome for a general user to run such a complex system. Modern systems have overcome this by the use of English-like command languages and interactive ways of command entry such as Graphic Users Interface (GUI).

6.2.3 Data

Geographic data and related tabular data can be collected in-house or purchased from a commercial data provider. The digital map forms the basic data input for GIS. Tabular data related to the map objects can also be attached to the digital data. A GIS will integrate spatial data with other data resources and can even use a DBMS, used by the most organization to maintain their data, to manage spatial data.

6.2.4 People

GIS users are ranged from technical specialists who design and maintain the system to those who use it to help them perform their everyday work. The people who use GIS can be broadly classified into two classes. The CAD/GIS operator's work is to vectorise the map objects. The use of this vectorised data to perform queries, analyses or any other work is the responsibility of a GIS engineer/user.

6.2.5 Method

Above all, a successful GIS operates according to a well-designed plan and business rules, which are the models and operating practices unique to each organization. There are various techniques used for map creation and further usage for any project. The map creation can either be automated raster to vector creator or it can be manually vectorised using the scanned images. The source of these digital maps can be either map prepared by any survey agency or satellite imagery.

CHAPTER SEVEN

GEOSPATIAL DATA FOR GIS

Learning Outcomes

On completion of this chapter students will be able to:

1. Recognize the data structures in GIS
2. Identify spatial and non-spatial data for GIS
3. Explain raster and vector data structures

7.1 Basics of geographical data

Geographical data are referenced to locations on the earth's surface by using a standard system of coordinates emanating from a particular projection system. Geographical data are very often recognised and described in terms of well-established geographical 'objects', or phenomenological concepts such as 'urban area', 'agricultural land', and 'forest' as fundamental building blocks for analysing and synthesising complex information.

Points, Lines, and Areas: All geographical data can be reduced to three basic topological concepts - the point, the line, and the area (Clarke, 1995). Every geographical phenomenon can in principle be represented by a point, line, or area plus a label saying what it is.

Map: A map is a set of points, lines, and areas that are defined both by their location in space with reference to a coordinate system and by their non-spatial attributes. The map legend is the key to linking the non-spatial attributes to the spatial entities. Non-spatial attributes may be indicated visually by colours, symbols, or shading, the meaning of which is defined in the legend. For GIS, non-spatial attributes need to be coded in a form in which they can be used for data analysis. A region is a set of pixels, areas, or polygons that are described by a single legend unit.

Basic map feature point, line, and area have different dimensions as described below:

- Points (0-D. no length or width)
- Lines (1-D, length, no width)
- Polygons/areas (2-D, length and width/area and perimeter)
- Surfaces (3-D Areas with Z Dimension)

Attribute data: Attribute data describes the characteristics of spatial features. These characteristics can be quantitative and/or qualitative in nature. Attribute data is often referred to as tabular data. The coordinate location of a forestry stand would be spatial data, while the characteristics of that forestry stand, e.g. cover group, dominant species, crown closure, height, etc., would be attribute data.

Image data: Image data ranges from satellite images and aerial photographs to scanned maps (maps that have been converted from print to digital format).

Metadata: It is a set of information that describes other data, like-

- scale
- accuracy
- projection/datum
- data source
- manipulations
- how to acquire data

7.2 Data model in GIS

In GIS data can be classified as (a) spatial data, (b) non-spatial data, and (c) Geo-referenced data (Figure 7.1). The coordinate location of a forestry stand would be spatial data, while the characteristics of that forestry stand, e.g. cover group, dominant species, crown closure, height, etc., would be attribute data. Other data types, in a particular image and multimedia data, are becoming more prevalent with changing technology. Depending on the specific content of the data, image data may be considered either spatial, e.g. photographs, animation, movies, etc., or attribute, e.g. sound, descriptions, narrations, etc.

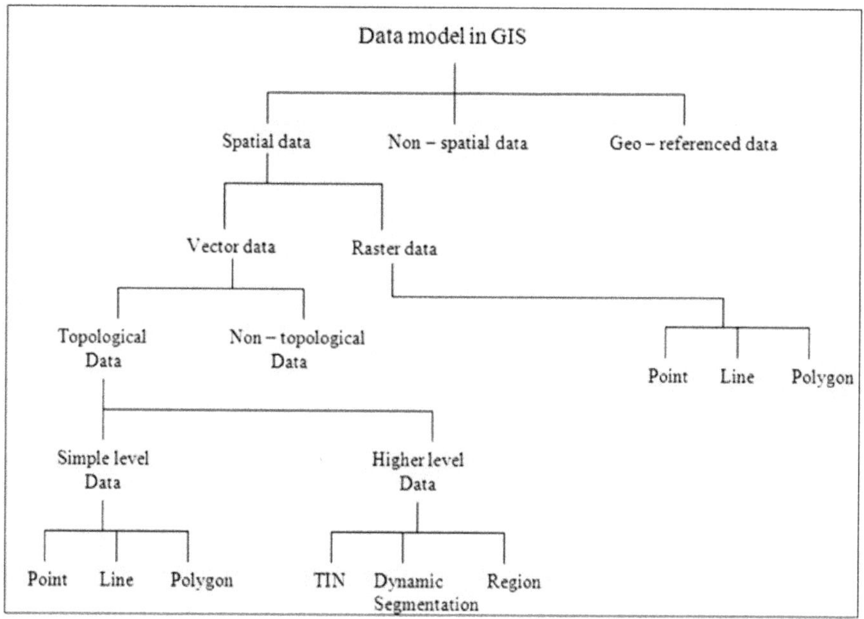

Figure 7.1 Data model in GIS

Traditionally spatial data has been stored and presented in the form of a map. Two basic types of spatial data have evolved for storing geographic data digitally. These are referred to as (1) Raster data and (2) Vector data (Figure 7.2). The following diagram reflects the two primary spatial data encoding techniques.

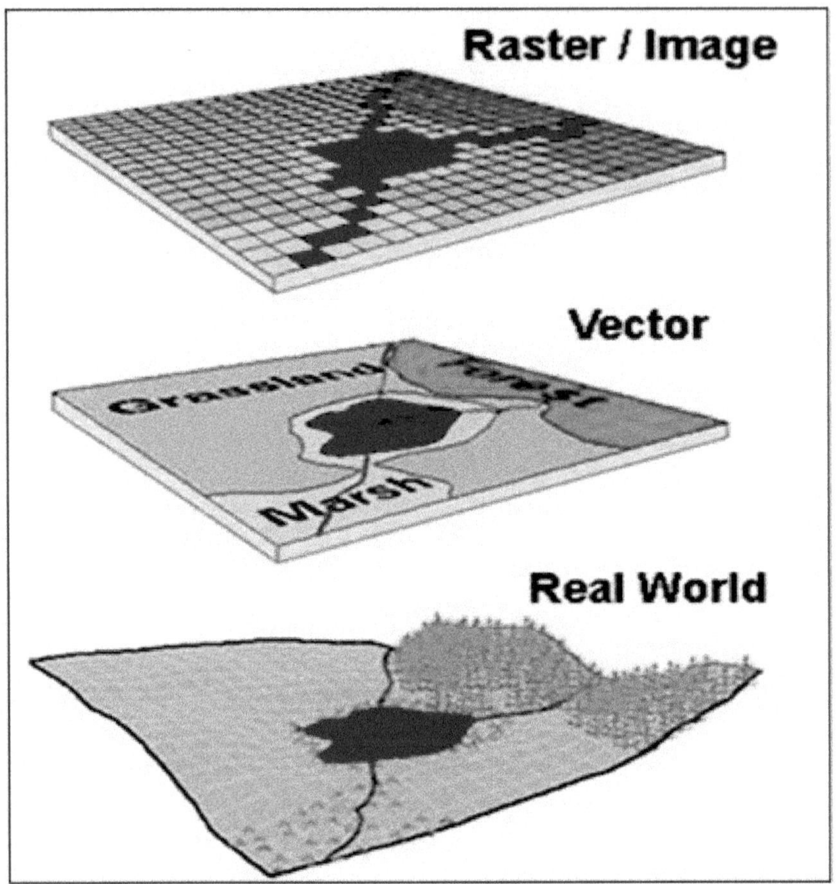

Figure 7.2 Raster vs. vector data structure

7.3 Raster data representation

The most straightforward raster data structures consist of an array of grid cells (or pixels). Each grid cell is referenced by a row and column number and it contains a number representing the type or value of the attribute being mapped. In raster structures a point is represented by a single grid cell; a line by a number of neighboring cells strung out in a given direction and an area by an agglomeration of neighboring cells (Figure7.3). The Basic map features point, line and area can be represented below:

- **Points:** Single cells, unique/known values;

- **Lines:** Strings of cells with common values;
- **Polygons/areas:** groups of cells with common values;

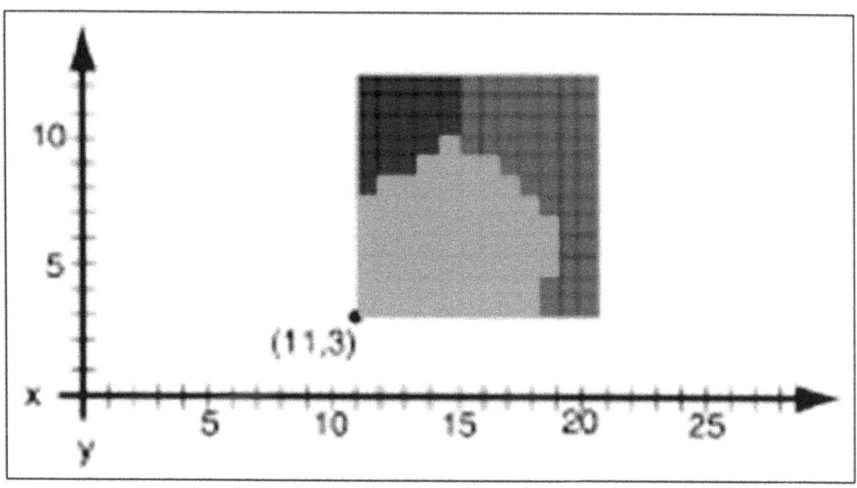

Figure 7.3 Raster data structure

7.4 Vector data representation

The vector representation of an object is an attempt to represent the object as exactly as possible. Point entities can be considered to embrace all geographical and graphical entities that are positioned by a single XY coordinate pair. Line entities can be defined as all linear fcatures built up of straight-line segments made up of two or more coordinates. Areas of polygons (or regions) can be represented in various ways in a vector database. The aim of a polygon data structure is to be able to describe the topological properties of areas (that is their shapes, neighbours and hierarchy) in such a way that the associated properties of these basic spatial building blocks can be displayed and manipulated as thematic map data. Vector Data is a discrete type of data represented by Cartesian coordinates (x, y). The Basic map features point, line and area can be represented below (Figure7.4).

- **Points:** id, x, y;
- **Lines:** id, x1,y1 ... xn, yn
- **Polygons:** id, x1,y1 ... xn, yn, where xn=x1, yn=y1 (closed)

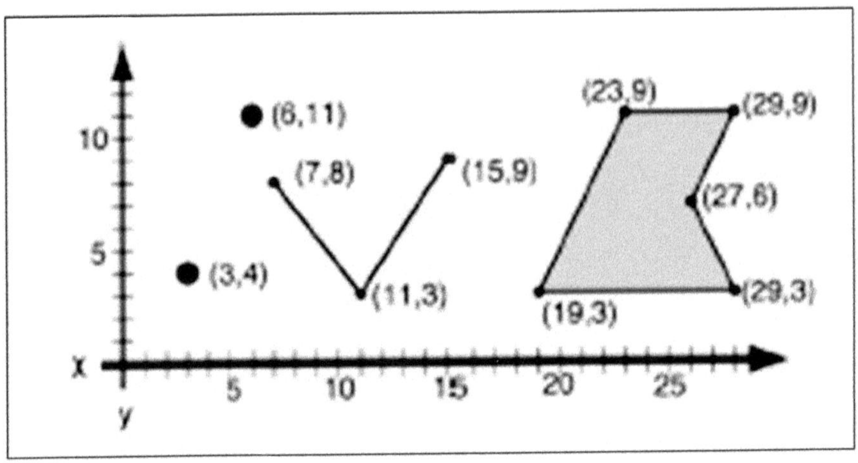

Figure 7.4 Vector data structure

7.5 Conversion of raster and vector data

Vector to Raster data conversion: The process of converting vector data, which is a series of points, lines, and polygons, into raster data, which is a series of cells each with a discrete value. This process is essentially easier than the reverse process, which is converting data from raster format to vector format.

Raster to vector conversion: The process of converting an image made up of raster cells into one described by vector data. This may or may not involve the encoding of topology.

7.6 Higher-level GIS data Structure

7.6.1Triangulated Irregular Network (TIN)

TIN is a surface representation derived from irregularly spaced points and break-line features. Each sample point has an x-y coordinate and a z value or surface value.

- The TIN model represents a surface as a set of contiguous, non-overlapping triangles. Within each triangle, the surface is represented by a plane.
- The triangles are made from a set of points called mass points. Mass points can occur at any location, the more carefully selected, the more accurate the model of the surface.

- Well-placed mass points occur where there is a major change in the shape of the surface, for example, at the peak of a mountain, the floor of a valley, or at the edge (top and bottom) of cliffs

The Delaunay Triangulation

Delaunay triangulation is a proximal method that satisfies the requirement that a circle drawn through the three nodes of a triangle will contain no other node (Watson and Philip, 1984; Tsai, 1993). Delaunay triangulation has several advantages over other triangulation methods:

- The triangles are as equiangular as possible, thus reducing potential numerical precision problems created by long skinny triangles
- Ensures that any point on the surface is as close as possible to a node
- The triangulation is independent of the order in the points are processed

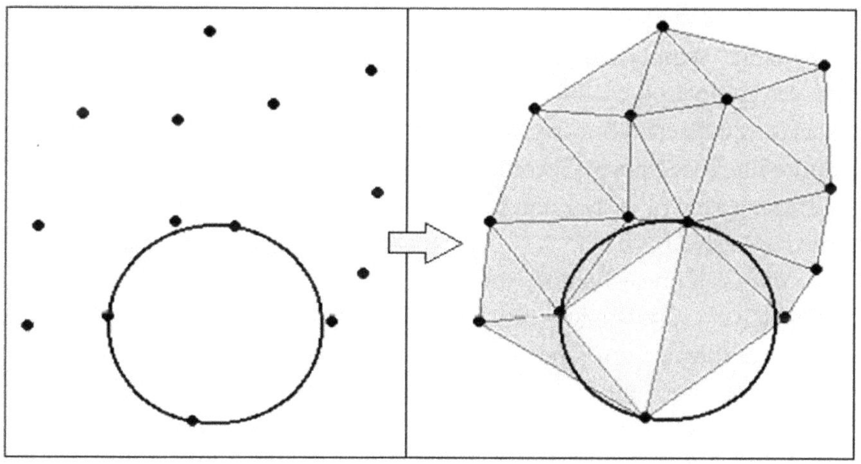

Figure 7.5 Construction of a TIN model from points

TINs from contours

Contours are a common source of digital elevation data. In general all the vertices of the contour lines are used as mass points for triangulation. In many cases this will cause the presence of flat triangles in the surface (Chang, 2018).

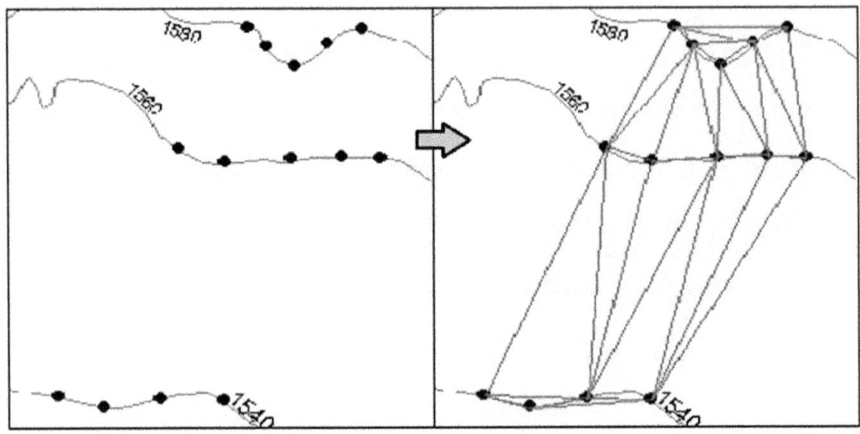

Figure 7.6 Construction of a TIN model from contours

7.6.2 Dynamic Segmentation

Dynamic segmentation is a two-step process performed on a spatial data set comprised of linear features. First, a route system is created by associating adjacent line segments with one or more groups that have a definite linear sequence. Second, descriptive information is associated with the routing system by referencing distances from the starting point of each route (Nyerges, 1990).

A route is a linear feature, such as a street, highway, or stream used in a GIS, which also has a linear measurement system stored with its geometry. Events are linearly referenced data, such as speed limits, traffic accidents, or fishery habitat conditions, which occur along routes (Chang, 2018).

7.6.3 Region

A region is a set of areas with similar geographic characteristics (Cleland et al., 1997). If a forest fire map is prepared using the concept of the region; the map will have two distinguishing features. Two or more regions can cover or overlap the same area burned by fires in different years or regions can include areas that are spatially disjoint (Chang, 2018).

The region may also follow type:

1. Uniform region: Geographic area with similar characteristics. Like- Landform region by classification of the slope, relief, soil, land use, etc.

2. Hierarchical region: Represent different spatial of hierarchy. Like- Administrative unit [Country – Province – district - ILG – village]

Based on spatial configuration regions are three types-

1. Contiguous region: Referred to a single polygon
2. Fragmented region: Referred to more than one polygon which is separated from each other.
3. Perforated region: Referred to one polygon with some other small region inside it.

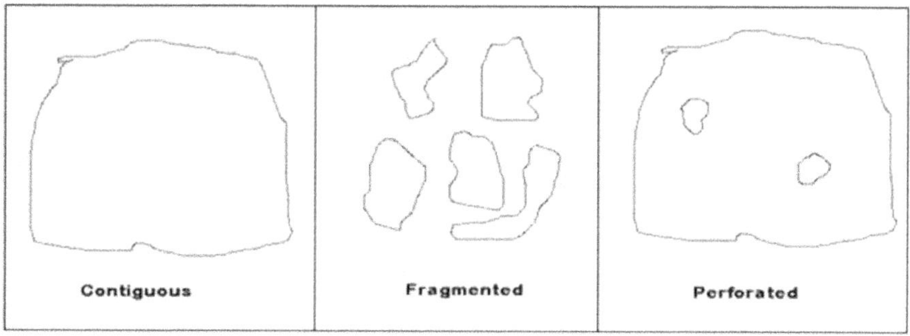

Figure 7.7 Different types of region

CHAPTER EIGHT

RASTER DATA AND VECTOR DATA MODEL

Learning Outcomes

On completion of this chapter students will be able to:

1. Recognize raster and vector-based in GIS
2. Explain the different formats of digital satellite imagery (raster)
3. Understand the topological relationship
4. Assess the advantages and disadvantages of raster and vector methods

8.1 Raster data model

Raster is a method for the storage, processing, and display of spatial data. Each area is divided into rows and columns, which form a regular grid structure with square cells. Each cell within this matrix contains location coordinates as well as an attribute value. The spatial location of each cell is implicitly contained within the ordering of the matrix, unlike a vector structure, which stores topology explicitly. The conventional sequence is row-by-row from the top left corner of the image or map. Each cell in the raster contains a single value, at least in modern raster GIS. This value can be a reference to another value, but the idea is that each cell has just a single value, and it is assumed that the value is distributed evenly throughout the cell. A raster GIS is space-filling since every location in the study area corresponds to a cell in the raster. One set of cells and associated values is a layer. There may be many layers in a database, e.g. soil type, elevation, and land use/land cover.

8.1.1 Elements of the raster data model

There are four (4) elements of a raster data model which are cell value, cell size, raster bands, and spatial reference.

Cell value: Each cell in a raster carries a value (Figure 8.1), which *represents the characteristic of a spatial phenomenon at the location* denoted by its row and column (Chang, 2018).

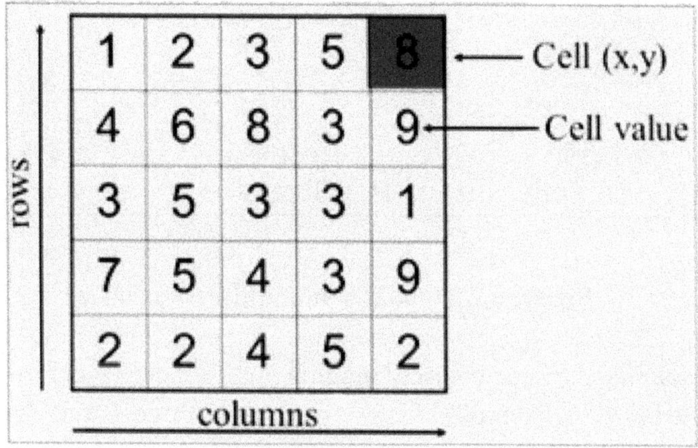

Figure 8.1 Cell value of a raster data

Cell size: In raster GIS the pixel equivalent is usually referred to as a cell element or grid cell. Pixel/cell refers to the smallest unit of information available in an image or raster map. This is the smallest element of a display device that can be independently assigned attributes such as colour. The level of detail (of features/phenomena) represented by a raster is often dependent on the cell (pixel) size of the raster. The cell must be small enough to capture the required detail but large enough so computer storage and analysis can be performed efficiently. More features, smaller features, or a greater detail in the extents of features can be represented by a raster with smaller cell size (Star and Estes, 1990). The size of the pixel must be half of the smallest distance to be represented (Figure 8.2).

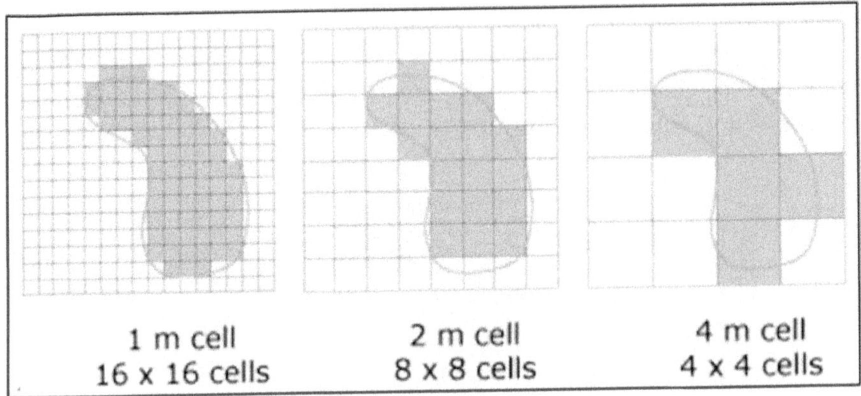

Figure 8.2 Comparison of different cell size

Raster bands: A raster dataset contains one or more layers called bands (Chang, 2018). For example, a color image has three bands (red, green, and blue) while a digital elevation model (DEM) has one band (holding elevation values), and a multispectral image may have many bands (Figure 8.3).

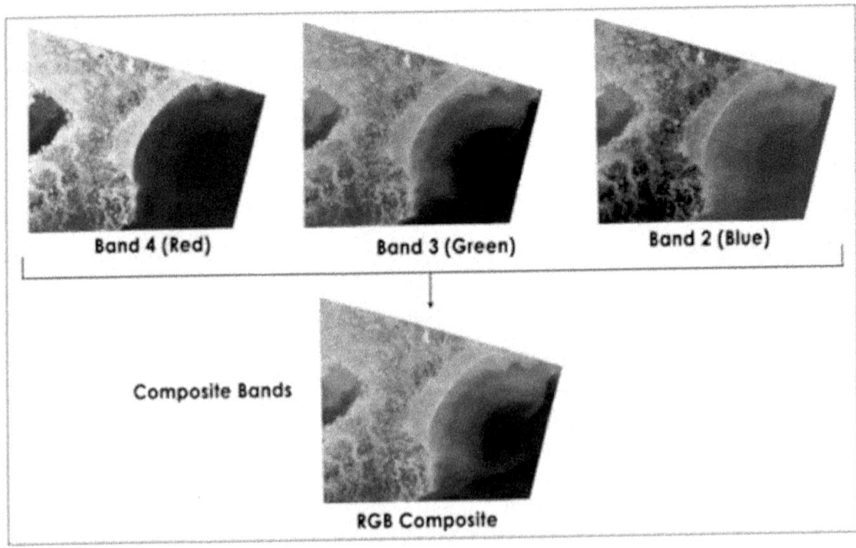

Figure 8.3 Multiple bands and RGB composite

Spatial reference: Spatial reference describes the projection system which links the raster data to a particular position on the earth's surface (Chang, 2018). Raster data must have spatial reference information so that they can align spatially with other data sets in a GIS (Figure 8.4).

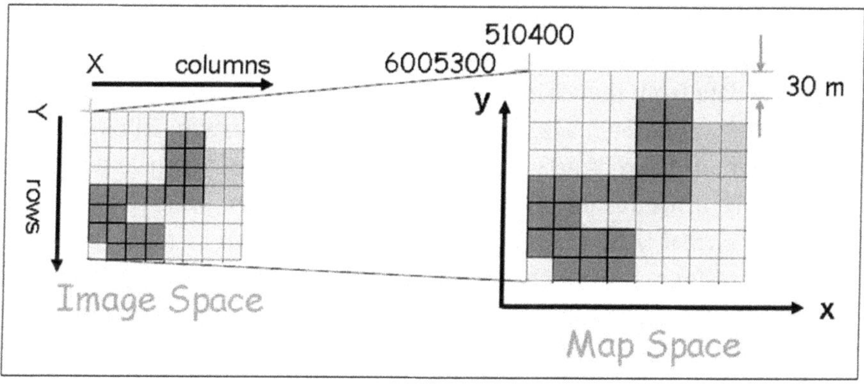

Figure 8.4 Multiple bands and RGB composite

8.1.2 Types of raster data

Raster data can be categorized into the following types

i. ***Satellite Imagery:*** Remotely sensed satellite data are recorded in raster format. The pixel value in a satellite image represents light energy reflected or emitted from the earth's surface.
ii. ***Digital Elevation Models (DEMs):*** A digital elevation model (DEM) consists of an array of uniformly spaced elevation data. A DEM is point-based, but it can easily be converted to raster data by placing each elevation point at the center of a cell.
iii. ***Binary Scanned Files:*** In this type of raster data a scanned image contains the value of 0 or 1.
iv. ***Digital Orthophotos (DOQ):*** A digital orthophoto quad (DOQ) is a digitized image prepared from aerial photographs or other remotely sensed data, in which the displacement caused by camera tilt and terrain relief has been removed. A digital orthophoto is geo-referenced and can be registered with topographic and other maps.

v. ***Graphic Files:*** In this type of raster data we can include maps, photographs, and images which can be stored as digital graphic files. Major popular graphic files in raster format are GIF (Graphic Interchange Format), TIFF (Tagged Image File Format), and JPEG (Joint Photographic Experts Group).

8.1.3 Data formats for digital satellite imagery

Digital data from the various satellite systems are supplied to the user in the form of computer-readable tapes, CD-ROM, USB drives, FTP transfers, or in the cloud. There is no worldwide standard for the storage and transfer of remotely sensed data. The CEOS (Committee on Earth Observation Satellites) format is of accepted as the standard. For an instance, an image consisting of four spectral channels can be visualised as four superimposed images, with corresponding pixels in one band registering exactly to those in the other bands.

There are three common methods of organizing image data for multiband images, namely (i) band sequential (BSQ), (ii) band interleaved by line (BIL), and (iii) Band interleaved by pixel (BIP). BIL, BIP, and BSQ are not in themselves image formats but are schemes for storing the actual pixel values of an image in a file.

Band Sequential (BSQ): Band sequential format stores information for the image one band at a time. In other words, data for all the pixels for band 1 is stored first, then data for all pixels for band 2, and so on (Figure 8.5). [Example: 1st row band1, 2nd row band1, 3rd row band1; 1st row band2, 2nd row band2, 3rd row band2, 1st row band3, 2nd row band3, 3rd row band3]

Band Interleaved by Line (BIL): Band interleaved by line data stores pixel information band-by-band for each line, or row, of the image. For example, given a three-band image, all three bands of data are written for row 1, all three bands of data are written for row 2, and so on (Figure 8.5)

[Example: 1st row band1, 1st row band2, 1st row band3; 2nd row band1, 2nd row band2, 2nd row band3; 3rd row band1, 3rd row band2, 3rd row band3]

Band Interleaved by Pixel (BIP): Band interleaved by pixel data is similar to BIL data, except that the data for each pixel is written band by band. For example, with the same three-band image, the data for bands 1, 2, and 3 are written for the first pixel in column 1; the data for bands 1, 2, and 3 are written for the first pixel in column 2; and so on (Figure 8.5).

[Example: 1st row 1st columnband1, 1st row 1st columnband2, 1st row 1st columnband3; 1^{st}row 2^{nd}columnband1, 1^{st}row 2^{nd}column band2, 1^{st}row 2^{nd}columnband3 and so on]

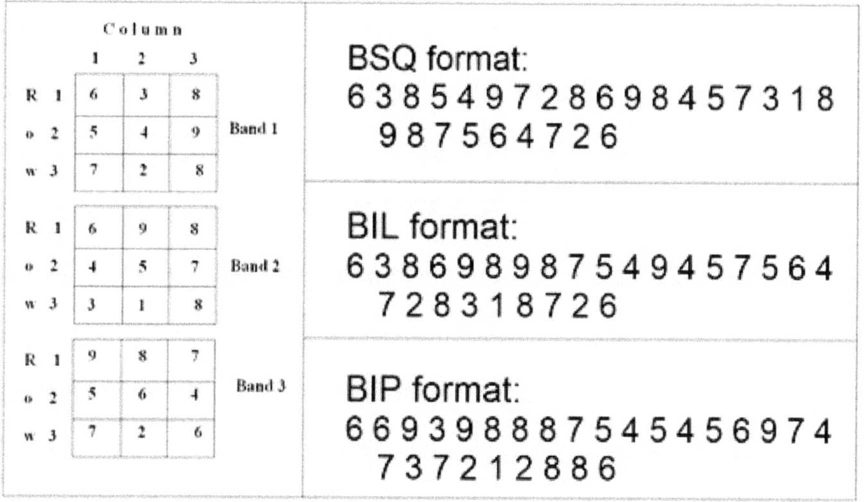

Figure 8.5 Example of BSQ, BIL and BIP image format

8.2 Vector data model

The vector representation of an object is an attempt to represent the object as exactly as possible. The coordinate space is assumed to be continuous, not quantized as with the raster space, allowing all positions, lengths, and dimensions to be defined precisely. Point entities can be considered to embrace all geographical and graphical entities that are positioned by a single XY coordinate pair. A vector-based GIS is defined by the vector representation of its geographic data. With the characteristics of this data model, geographic objects are explicitly represented and, within the spatial characteristics, the thematic aspects are associated. There are different ways of organising this double database (spatial and thematic). Usually, vector systems are composed of two components: the one that manages spatial data and the one that manages thematic data. This is a sort of hybrid organisation system, as it links a relational database for the attributes with a topological one for the spatial data. A key element in these kinds of systems is the identifier of every object. This identifier is unique and different for each object and allows the system to connect both databases.

Vector data models can be structured in many different ways. Two important data models namely (i) simple vector data model or Spaghetti data model and (ii) topological data model are described in the next.

8.2.1 Spaghetti data model

The vector data model uses the geometric objects of point, line, and area to represent simple spatial features. The simplest vector data structure is called the spaghetti data model (Dangermond, 1982). In the spaghetti model, each point, line, and/or polygon feature is represented as a string of X, Y coordinate pairs (Figure 8.6). Line entities can be defined as all linear features built up of straight line segments made up of two or more coordinates. Areas of polygons (or regions) can be represented in various ways in a vector database. The aim of a polygon data structure is to be able to describe the topological properties of areas (that is their shapes, neighbors, and hierarchy) in such a way that the associated properties of these basic spatial building blocks can be displayed and manipulated as thematic map data.

Despite the location designations associated with each line, or strand of spaghetti, spatial relationships are not explicitly encoded within the spaghetti model; rather, they are implied by their location. This results in a lack of topological information, which is problematic if the user attempts to make measurements or analyses.

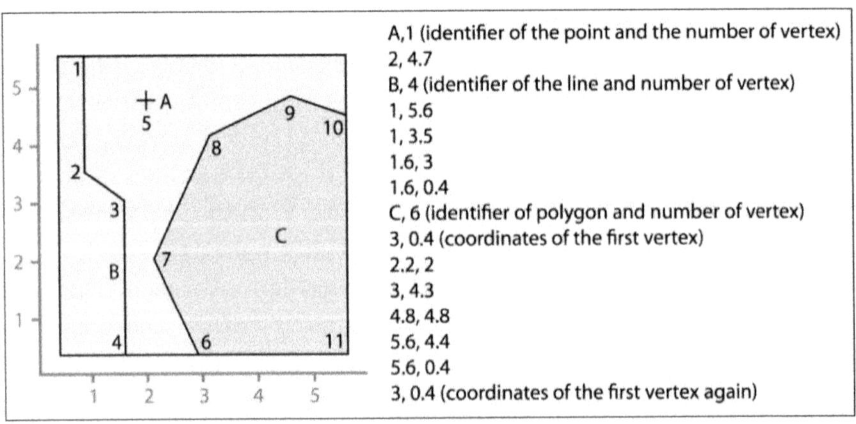

Figure 8.6 Spaghetti data model/ simple vector data model

8.2.2 Topological data model

The topological data model describes the topological information within the dataset in comparison to the spaghetti data model. Topology refers to sets of rules and behaviors that model how features share geometry. It also describes the relationships between neighboring points, lines, and polygons (Wilson and Watkins 1991) in a vector-based GIS.

Topology in the TIGER ***(Topologically Integrated Geographic Encoding and Referencing)*** (Figure 8.7) database involves 0-cells or points, 1-cells or line, and 2-cells or areas (Cooke, 1998).

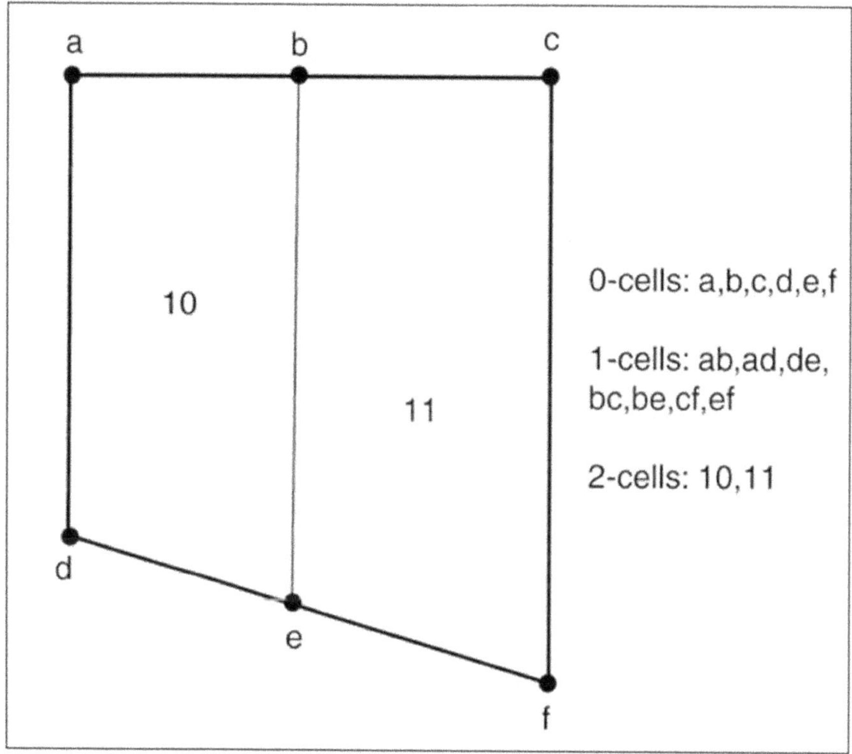

Figure 8.7 Topology in the TIGER database

There are three topological principles that need to be elaborated to understand the topological vector data model (Environmental Systems Research Institute, Inc., 1998), namely (i) connectivity, (ii) area definition, and (iii) contingency.

(i) Connectivity: It describes the relationship between arc and node (arc-node topology) in the vector-based GIS. In the topological data model, nodes are not only simple points, but they are the intersection points where two or more arcs meet. In an arc-node topology, the from-node is the starting node, from where the arc begins and ends up at a to-node or ending node (Figure 8.8).

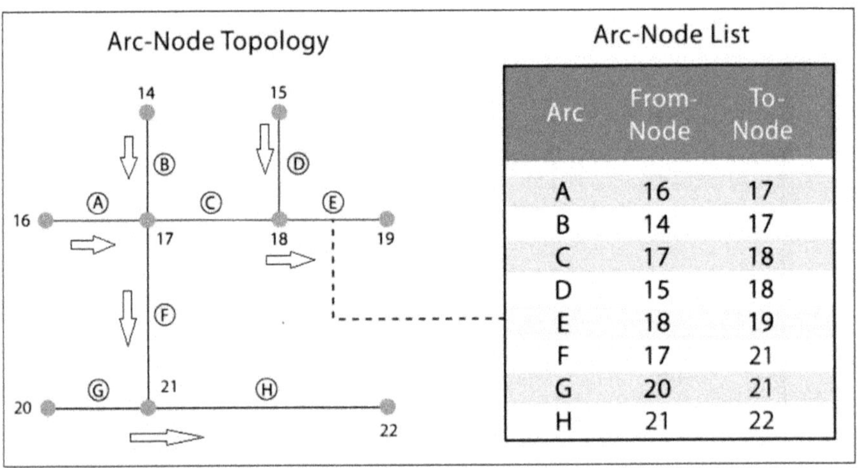

Arc	From-Node	To-Node
A	16	17
B	14	17
C	17	18
D	15	18
E	18	19
F	17	21
G	20	21
H	21	22

Figure 8.8 Arc-node topology

(ii) Area definition: It describes about the spatial relationship between polygon and arc. The relationship is called polygon-arc topology. Arcs are generally used to construct polygons. One polygon can be made of many arcs. On the other hand, it can be stated that one arc can be a common/ shared boundary of two adjacent polygons (Figure 8.9).

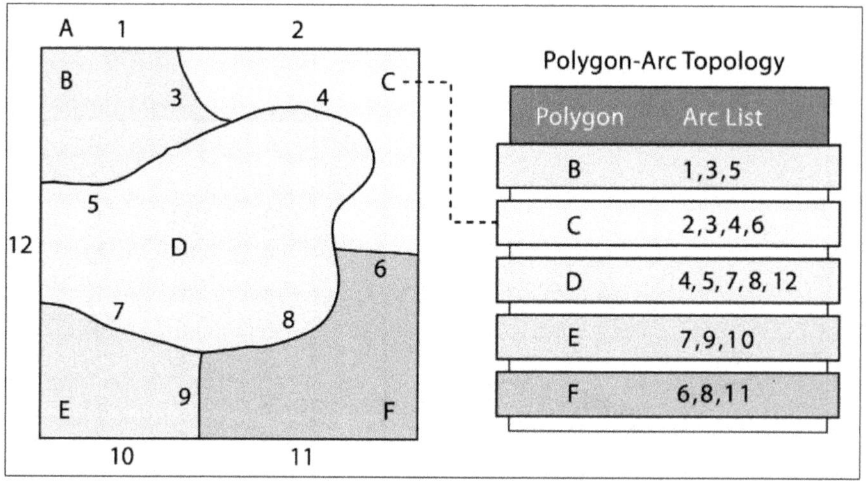

Figure 8.9 ThePolygon-arc topology

(iii) Contingency: It pronounces the spatial relationship between two polygons who shares a common or adjacent boundary. Polygon topology is important where all arcs have a specific direction (From node and to node) and are used to construct polygon features. In this way, the polygons situated on the “left” and “right” side of each arc can be demarcated (Figure 8.10).

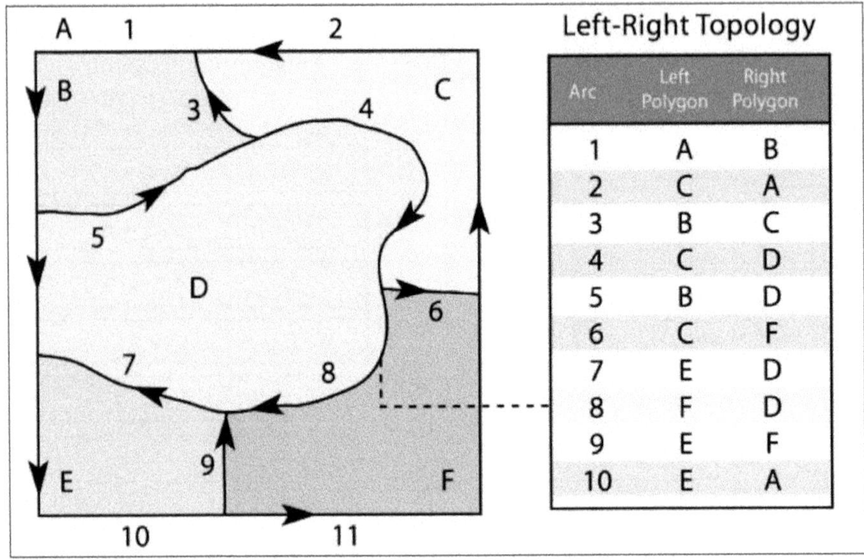

Left-Right Topology

Arc	Left Polygon	Right Polygon
1	A	B
2	C	A
3	B	C
4	C	D
5	B	D
6	C	F
7	E	D
8	F	D
9	E	F
10	E	A

Figure 8.10 Topology of polygon

8.3 Choice of Data Model: Advantages and Disadvantages

The essential differences between the two approaches are how they deal with representing things in space. Raster systems are built on the premise that there is something at all points of interest, so we will record something for every location. The space under consideration is exhausted by a regular data structure. The concern is not with the boundaries between objects as much as with the objects themselves, their interiors, or the phenomena they are representing. Spatial resolution is not as important as complete coverage.

Vector systems are built on the premise that we only need to record and deal with the essential points. If there isn't something of significance at a location, don't record anything. Not all locations in space are referenced, and many are simply referenced indirectly, as being inside a polygon. The data structure supports irregular objects and very high resolution. We are interested in the boundaries between objects at least as much as with the objects themselves, often more so. We need the precision representation of linear objects, and this need overrides other needs for surface and area modeling of all but the simplest kind. Precision is the watchword in vector GIS, together with making spatial relationships explicit.

The explicit nature of the relationships in vector GIS requires 'topology', which we will examine in a moment. It also allows much easier analysis of these kinds of relationships, especially connectivity between locations (points), which is done with lines. In raster GIS, we can figure out which cells are the eight surrounding the one we are currently in, so connectivity is implicit in the data structure, and we don't need all this extra stuff.

Acceptability of raster and vector data models with Quantification

Entity / Operation	Raster	Vector	**Raster**	**Vector**
Precision in graphics	✗	✓	7	3
Traditional cartography	✗	✓	7	3
Data volume	✗	✓	7	3
Topology	✗	✓	7	3
Computation	✓	✗	3	7
Update	✓	✗	3	7
Continuous space	✓	✗	3	7
Integration	✓	✗	3	7
Discontinuous	✗	✓	7	3

Advantages and disadvantages of raster methods

Advantages	**Disadvantages**
✦ Simple data structure ✦ The overlay and combination of mapped data with remotely sensed data is easy ✦ Various kinds of spatial analysis are easy ✦ The technology is cheap	✦ Volumes of graphic data ✦ The use of large cells to reduce data volumes means there can be a serious loss of information ✦ Network linkages are difficult to establish ✦ Crude raster maps are considered to be less beautiful.

Advantages and disadvantages of vector methods

Advantages	Disadvantages
✚ Good representation of phenomenological data structure	✚ Complex data structure
✚ Compact data structure ✚ Topology can be completely described with network linkages	✚ Display and plotting can be expensive, particularly for high quality, colour and cross-hatching.
✚ Accurate graphics	✚ The technology is expensive, particularly for the more sophisticated software.
✚ Retrieval, updating and generalisation of graphics and attributes are possible	✚ Spatial analysis and filtering within polygons are difficult.

CHAPTER NINE

GIS DATA INPUT, ATTRIBUTE DATA MODEL AND GIS APPLICATIONS

Learning Outcomes

On completion of this chapter students will be able to:

1. Identify different methods of data input into the GIS
2. Understand the attribute data model
3. Evaluate the capabilities and applications of geographic information system

9.1 GIS data input

Data input is the operation of encoding the data and writing them to the database. Two aspects of data have to be considered separately for GIS, viz., the positional or geographical data necessary to define where the graphic or cartographic features occur and the associated attributes that record what the cartographic features represent (Burrough and McDonnell, 2015). Data input to a GIS can be subdivided into few as below:

A. Entering the spatial data (digitizing): The choice of the method of entering spatial data is highly dependent upon the application, the available budget, and the type of data being input (Longley et al., 2015). The types of data include existing maps, aerial photographs, remote sensing data, census data, etc. The actual method of data input is also dependent upon the structure of the geographical system.

(1) Manual input to a vector system: Here the source data are envisaged as points, lines, or areas. The coordinates of the data are obtained from the reference grid already on the map or from the reference to a graticule or overlaid grid. The values can be simply fed into a computer.

(2) Manual input to a grid system: Here all points, lines, and areas are envisaged assets of cells. The most straightforward and most tedious method includes the selection of grid cell (raster) of appropriate size. Now a transparent grid of that size is laid over the map. The values of a single map attribute for each cell are then written down and fed into the computer.

(3) Digitizing: The enormous labor of writing down the coordinates and then typing them into a file on a computer can be reduced by using a digitizer to encode the X and Y coordinates of the desired points, lines, areas, or grid cells. A digitizer is an electronic device consisting of a tablet upon which the map or document can be placed. Lines can be digitized in two ways; stream digitizing and point digitizing. In-stream digitizing, the cursor is placed at the beginning of the line, and a command is set in the computer to start recording coordinates at either equal intervals of time or equal intervals in the X or Y direction and the operator moves the cursor along the line. At the end or at a junction, the computer stops accepting points. The rate at which coordinates are recorded depends upon the speed with which the operator can trace the line. A digitizer can be used to input the vector data (points, lines, and the boundaries of areas), by entering the coordinates of the entities.

(4) Automated scanning: To handle a lot of data in less time, we have to go for quicker alternatives than digitizers (i.e, scanners). Scanners can be of two types; raster scanners and vector scanners. Raster scanners work on the principle that a point or any part of the map may have one or two colours, black or white. Raster output can be converted to vector form by thinning algorithms. The alternative to scanning lines using a raster device and then restoring the vector structure by brute force can be substituted by vector scanning.

B. Entering non-spatial associated attributes: Non-spatial associated attributes (feature codes) are those properties of a spatial entity that need to be handled in the GIS. For example, a road can be digitized as a set of continuous pixels, or as a vector line entity. The road can be represented in the spatial part of the GIS by a certain colour, symbol, or data location. Data about the type of road (motorway or unmetalled road) can be included.

All these data represent one common entity, road, which can be stored and processed apart from spatial data. By giving each type of data a common identifier they can be efficiently linked in any desired way.

C. **Linking spatial and non-spatial data:** This requires that the digital representations of the points, lines, and areas carry unique identifiers. Both the identifier and the coordinate are thus stored in the database. Once the spatial and non-spatial data have been input, the linkage operation provides an ideal operation to verify the quality of both types of data.

9.2 Attribute data model

9.2.1 Attribute data

Attribute data in GIS are stored in tables. An attribute table is organized by row and column. Each row represents a spatial feature, each column describes a characteristic, and the intersection of a column and a row shows the value of a particular characteristic for a particular feature. A row is also called a record, and a column is also called a field (Figure 9.1). There are two types of attribute tables for vector data in GIS (Chang, 2018). The first type is the feature attribute table, which has access to the feature geometry. Every vector data set has a feature attribute table. In the case of the geo-relational data model, the feature attribute table uses the feature ID to link to the feature's geometry. This second type of attribute table is non-spatial, meaning that the table does not have direct access to the feature geometry but has a field linking the table to the feature attribute table whenever necessary (Chang, 2018).

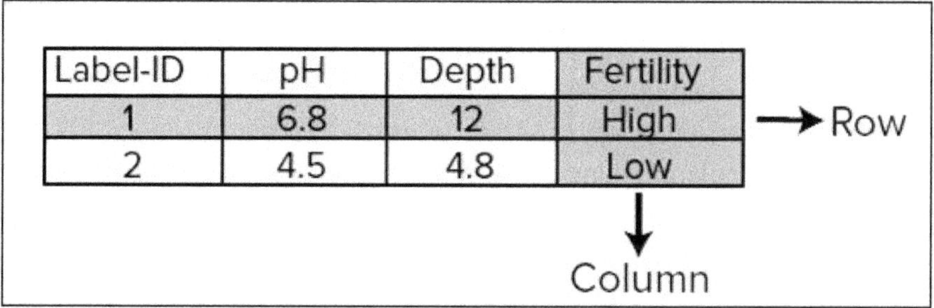

Label-ID	pH	Depth	Fertility
1	6.8	12	High
2	4.5	4.8	Low

Figure 9.1 A feature attribute table consists of rows and columns

9.2.2 Databases management

The presence of feature attributes and non-spatial data tables means that a GIS requires a database management system (DBMS) to manage these tables. A DBMS is a software package that enables us to build and manipulate a database (Oz, 2004). A DBMS provides tools for data input, search, retrieval, manipulation, and output.

9.2.3 Types of attribute data

There are different types of attribute data that can be stored in a table or database (Chang, 2018) as below:

- ***Character/String:*** It is text-based value; sometime rank can be attached to it (A to Z or A1, etc.)
- ***Integer:*** Numbers without decimal digits (2, 5, 10, 15, and 50)
- ***Real value/floating point:*** Numbers with decimal digits (2.1, 5.25, and 10.5)
- ***Date:*** Description of day/month/year
- ***BLOB:*** Binary large object stores images, multimedia, and feature geometrics with 0s and 1s.

9.2.4 Type of attribute data according to measurement scale (Stevens, 1946)

- ***Nominal*** *(Character):* It concerns values that represent different kinds or different categories of data (Land use type, soil type etc)
- ***Ordinal*** *(Character):* It concerns measurements that quantify differences by order (ie. in terms of values such as 'more' or 'less', 'larger' or 'smaller' often used where quantitative differences are apparent but hard to measure.
- ***Interval*** *(Integer or Float):* Data with known intervals between values (a temperature reading of 70°F is warmer than 60°Fby 10°F)
- ***Ratio*** *(Numerical type):* Same as interval one but meaning full and absolute (Population densities, where density of 0 is an absolute zero)

9.2.5 Types of Relationships

In the GIS database four types of relationships are found between/among the data (Chang, 2018) as (Figure 9.2) below:

- ***One-to-one***: one record in a table is related to another record in another table.
- ***One-to-many***: one record in a table may be related to many records in another table. (Street address of an apartment complex may include

several households)

- ***Many-to-one:*** Many records in a table may be related to one record in another table (Several households may share the same street address).
- ***Many-to-many:*** Many records in a table may be related to many records in another table.

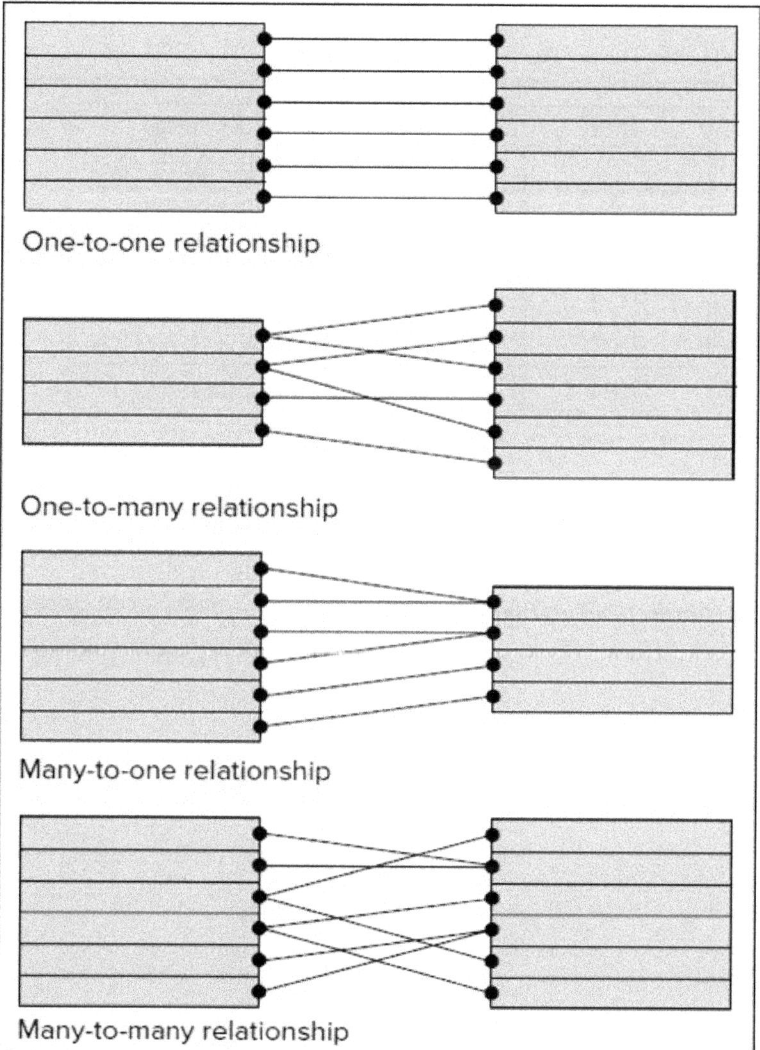

Figure 9.2 Types of relationship in GIS

9.2.5 Attribute Data Model types

Different attribute data models are used to store, manipulate, analyse and maintain attribute data for GIS software. The most common data models (Chang, 2018) are (i) Tabular data model ("flat file"), (ii) Hierarchical data model, (iii) Network data model, and (iv) Relational attribute data model.

(i) Tabular data model ("flat file"): Tabular data model ("flat file") or a flat file containing all the data in a large table. A feature attribute table is like a flat file. Another example is a spreadsheet with data only (Figure 9.3).

PIN	Owner	Zoning
P101	Wang	Residential (1)
P101	Chang	Residential (1)
P102	Smith	Commercial (2)
P102	Jones	Commercial (2)
P103	Costello	Commercial (2)
P104	Smith	Residential (1)

Figure 9.3 Tabular or flat file

(ii) Hierarchical attribute data model: A hierarchical database organizes its data at different levels and uses only one-to-many associations between levels (Figure 9.4).

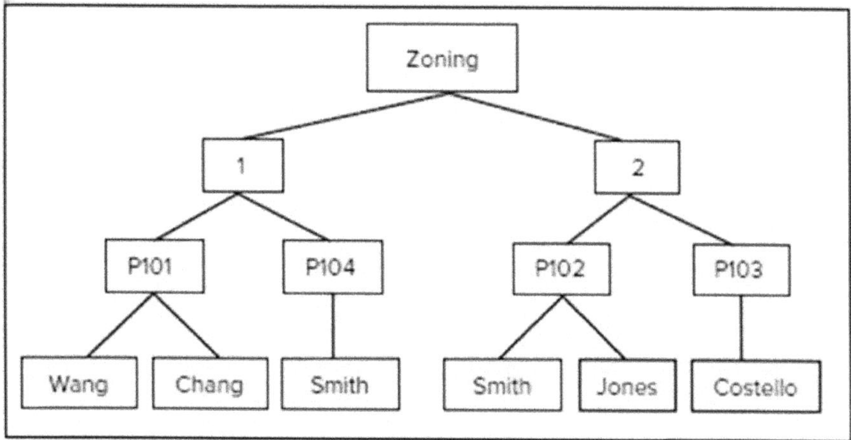

Figure 9.4 Hierarchical attribute data model

(iii) Network attribute data model: A network database builds connections across the tables as shown in figure 9.5.

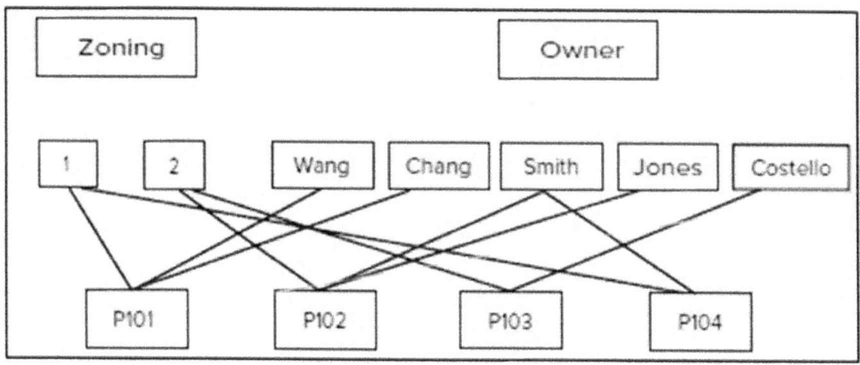

Figure 9.5 Network attribute data model

(iv) Relational attribute data model: A relational database is collection of tables, also called relations which can be connected with each other by key (Figure 9.6 & 9.7).

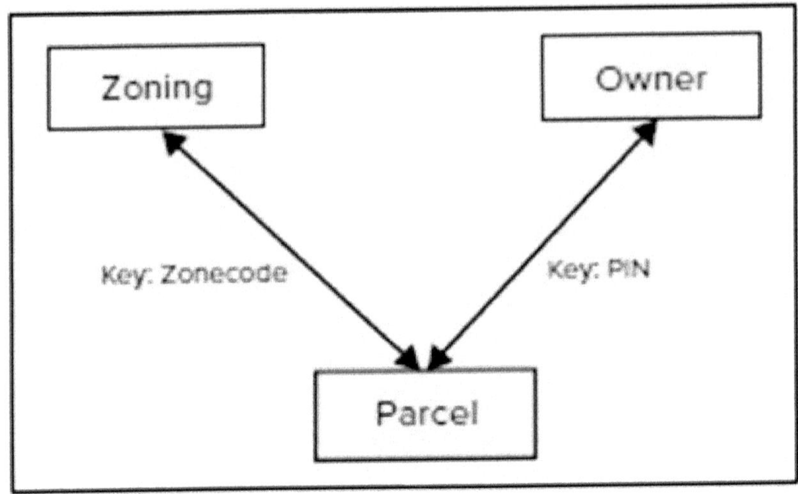

Figure 9.6 Relational attribute data model

Primary key

Record	Soil-ID	Area	Perimeter
1	1	106.39	495.86
2	2	8310.84	508,382.38
3	3	554.11	13,829.50
4	4	531.83	19,000.03
5	5	673.88	23,931.47

Foreign key

Soil-ID	suit	soilcode
1	1	Id3
2	3	Sg
3	1	Id3
4	1	Id3
5	2	Ns1

Origin ← Destination

Figure 9.7 Relational attribute data model with primary and foreign key

9.3 GIS applications

Geographic Information Systems (GIS) can be used in various fields including Mapping, Urban Planning, Transportation Planning, etc. Few applications are highlighted below:

- **Mapping locations:** GIS can be used to map locations. GIS allows the creation of maps through automated mapping, data capture, and surveying analysis tools.

- **Mapping quantities:** People map quantities, like where the most and least are, to find places that meet their criteria and take action, or to see the relationships between places. This gives an additional level of information beyond simply mapping the locations of features.
- **Mapping densities:** While you can see concentrations by simply mapping the locations of features, in areas with many features it may be difficult to see which areas have a higher concentration than others. A density map lets you measure the number of features using a uniform areal unit, such as acres or square miles, so you can clearly see the distribution.
- **Finding distances:** GIS can be used to find out what's occurring within a set distance of a feature.
- **Mapping and monitoring change:** GIS can be used to map the change in an area to anticipate future conditions, decide on a course of action, or evaluate the results of an action or policy.

CHAPTER TEN

GLOBAL NAVIGATION SATELLITE SYSTEM

Learning Outcomes

On completion of this chapter students will be able to:

1. Understand the basics of the global navigation satellite system (GNSS)
2. Illustrate various satellite constellations leading to GNSS
3. Explain different augmentation systems in GNSS

10.1 Global navigation satellite system (GNSS)

GNSS is the terminology given to all constellations of Satellite Positioning, Navigation, and Time (PNT) for many applications on and above the Earth's surface. GNSS includes the major universal satellite systems and as well as the Regional/National Satellite Systems known as Satellite Based Augmentation Systems (SBAS) that are mainly produced signals to assist the Global Positioning System (GPS) for improvement of the quality, integrity, and availability of satellite signals, especially for the safety of life on navigation on approach mainly on airports around the globe. Galileo and BEIDOU Compass are progressing into the global stage with satellite launching and structuring their orbit locations in space to be compatible with other systems for integration into one extensive universal system of Satellite Constellation to be known as the Global Navigation Satellite System (GNSS).

10.2 GNSS constellation

Receivers receive signals which are generated from constellations satellites orbiting around the Earth in several planes. Signals from four satellites can determine any position on or above the Earth's surface. GPS and GNSS work together, but the GNSS is more reliable and accurate than GPS. GNSS-compatible equipment generally uses navigational satellites from another network that is beyond the GPS system. The four major GNSS constellations are outlined in table 10.1 with their operational satellites, orbital information, owner, and services.

Table 10.1 Four major GNSS constellations (CASA, 2006)

GNSS	GPS	BEIDOU	Galileo	GLONASS
Operational satellites (2020)	31	35	24	24
Orbital height (km)	20,200 km	GEO: 35,786 km MEO:21,528 km	23,222 km	19,100 km
Owner/operator	United States, Department of Defense (DOD)	China National Space Administration	European Union	Russia, Russian Space Forces
Service	The two levels of service provided are known as the standard positioning service (SPS) and the precise positioning service (PPS). Horizontal positioning accuracy of 36 meters PPS is more accurate than SPS, but is available only to the US military	The open service provides free location, velocity and timing data, with positioning accuracy of 10 meters, velocity accuracy of 0.2 meters/second and timing accuracy of 10 nanoseconds.	The constellation is planned to have a bigger footprint than GPS, with 30 satellites. Accuracy is an average 8 meters horizontal and 9 meters vertical, 95 per cent of the time.	Same as GPS and is also based on a constellation of orbiting satellites and a ground control segment. Horizontal positioning accuracy within 5–10 meters and vertical positioning within 15 meters.

10.3 Augmentation systems

Augmentation is a system that helps GPS by providing accuracy, integrity, availability, or any other improvement to positioning, navigation, and timing which are not inherently part of GPS itself. A number of augmentation systems can be used to improve the navigational performance provided by the GNSS constellations. Table 10.2 contains ICAO-recognized different types of augmentation systems used in Australia.

Table 10.2 Types of augmentation systems used in Australia (CASA, 2006)

Type of augmentation	Benefits
Aircraft-based augmentation system (ABAS)	Resolves integrity deficiencies.
Satellite-based augmentation system (SBAS)	Provides third-party monitoring of GNSS ranging signals and broadcasts corrections over a wide area from a communications satellite, with a moderate improvement in accuracy.
Ground-based augmentation system (GBAS)	Provides third-party monitoring of GNSS ranging signals and broadcasts corrections over a local area from a ground station. GBAS provides a large improvement in accuracy and clears the way for the GNSS precision approach and landing.

10.3.1 Aircraft-based augmentation system (ABAS)

Aircraft-based augmentation systems (ABAS) use onboard equipment designed to overcome the performance limitations of the GNSS constellations. Current ABAS stand-alone receivers are designed to resolve integrity deficiencies. Highly integrated systems may use other aids such as inertial navigation. Aircraft-based augmentation system is positioned with six satellites to support fault detection and exclusion (Figure 10.1).

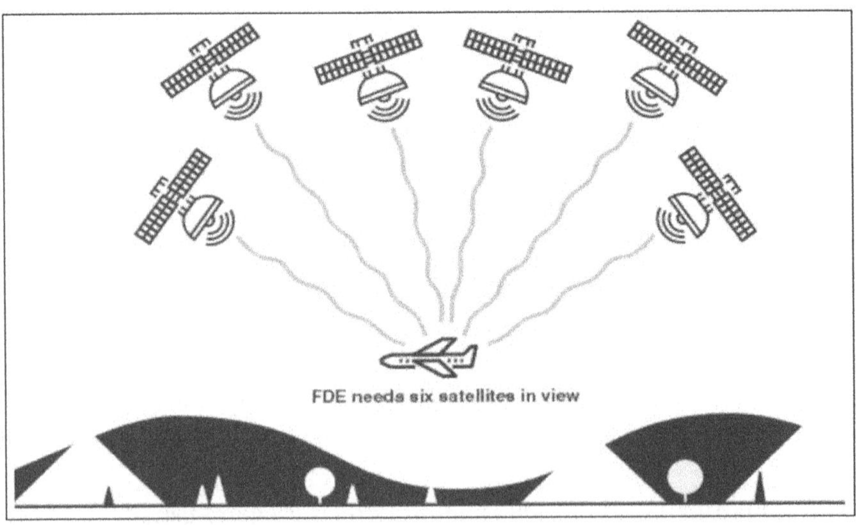

Figure 10.1 Example of Aircraft-based augmentation system

The two ABAS currently in use are (a) receiver autonomous integrity monitoring (RAIM) and the (b) aircraft autonomous integrity monitor (AAIM). Table 10.3 explains the different capabilities of RAIM and AAIM.

Table 10.3 Capabilities of RAIM and AAIM (CASA, 2006)

RAIM	AAIM
RAIM ensures that: i. An erroneous ranging signal from a satellite will not adversely affect the accurate navigation of the aircraft ii. The constellation geometry is good enough to provide an accurate position—that is, the satellites are spread evenly across the sky iii. If an error is detected within the constellation, pilots are notified that they cannot rely on GNSS for navigation.	Aircraft autonomous integrity monitor (AAIM) uses i. The redundancy of position estimates from multiple sensors, including GNSS, to provide integrity performance that is at least equivalent to RAIM. ii. AAIM uses inertial navigation solutions as an integrity check of the GPS solution when RAIM is unavailable, but GPS positioning information continues to be valid.

RAIM unavailability or outages or holes, are times when there are too few satellites with the appropriate spacing for integrity monitoring.

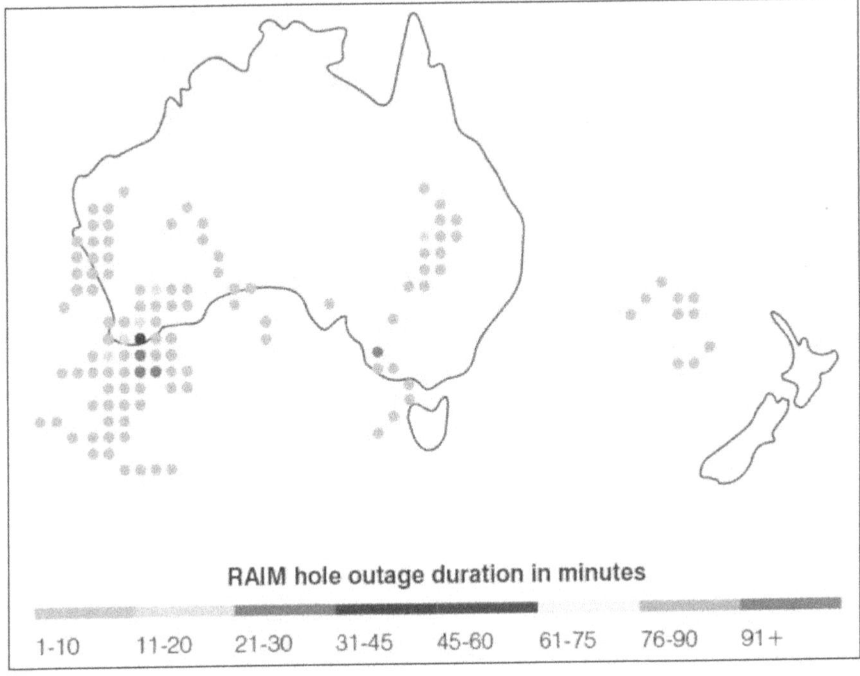

Figure 10.2 RAIM outage map of Australia

10.3.2 Satellite-based augmentation system (SBAS)

The SBAS supports regional augmentation by using additional satellite-broadcast messages like ranging, integrity, and tracking signals. Geostationary satellites which are orbiting earth from 36000 km appear to be stationed at any point on the Erath surface and are owned and operated independently of the GNSS constellations (Figure 10.3).

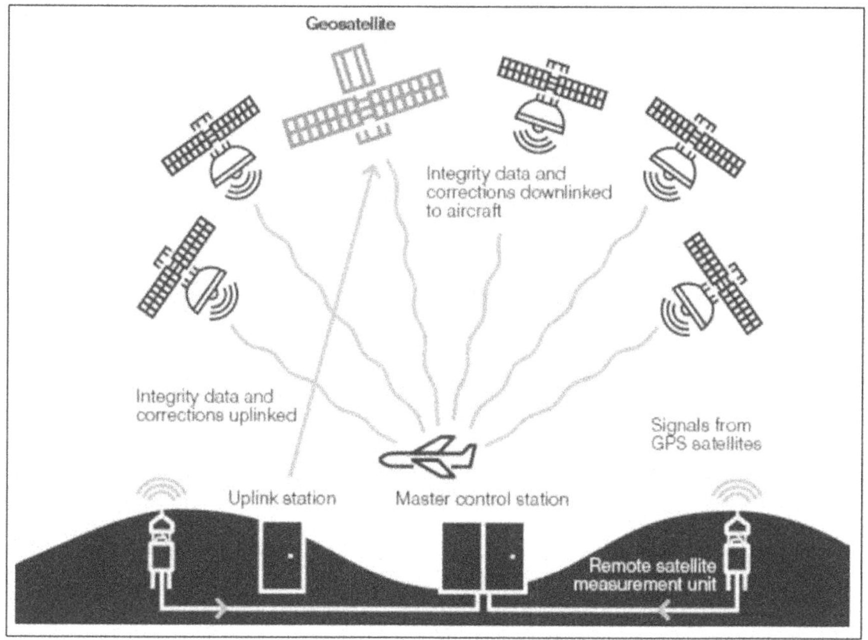

Figure 10.3 Satellite-based augmentation systems

The SBAS system comprises (a) a network of ground reference stations that monitor satellite signals, (b) master stations that collect and process reference station data and generate SBAS messages, (c) uplink stations that send the messages to geostationary satellites, and (d) transponders on these satellites that broadcast the SBAS messages (Figure 10.3).

10.3.3 Ground-based augmentation system (GBAS)

GBAS provide GPS integrity monitoring through data obtained from the ground (Figure 10.4).

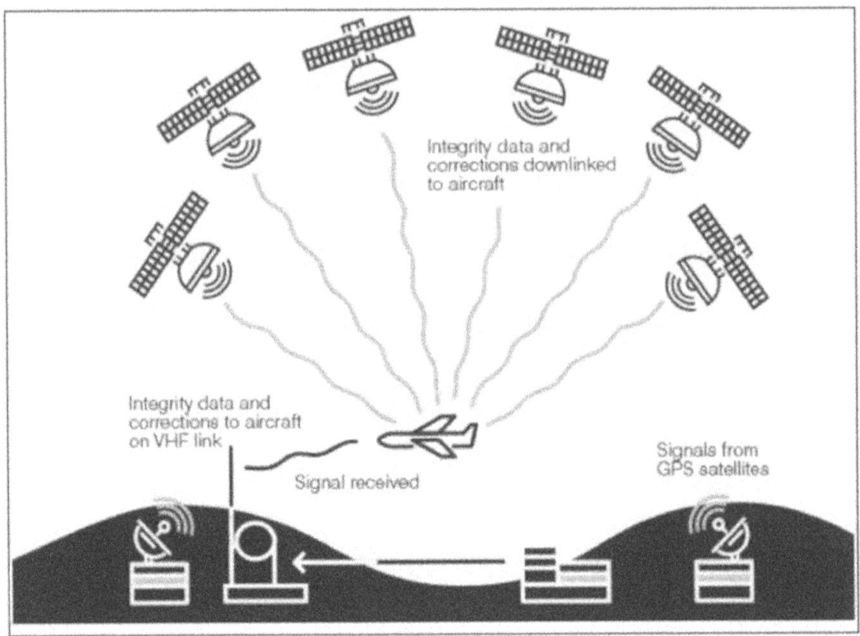

Figure 10.4 Ground-based augmentation systems

They also boost the accuracy of satellite navigation, clearing the way for GNSS precision approach and landing. An airport ground station transmits locally relevant corrections, integrity data, and approach data to aircraft in the terminal area in the VHF band.

A system meeting ICAO's GBAS requirements provides two services (i) precision approach service and (ii) GBAS positioning service. The ***precision approach service*** provides deviation guidance for GNSS landing system (GLS) approaches. A GBAS installation will typically provide GNSS corrections that support precision approaches to multiple runways at a single airport. A ***GBAS positioning service*** could provide horizontal position, velocity, and time information to support area navigation (RNAV) operations in terminal areas, though no such services are currently in use.

CHAPTER ELEVEN

INTRODUCTION TO GLOBAL POSITIONING SYSTEM

Learning Outcomes

On completion of this chapter students will be able to:

1. Understand the basics of global positioning system (GPS)
2. Illustrate different components/segments of GPS
3. Identify different applications of GPS

11.1 Introduction to GPS

A global Positioning System (GPS) is a radio navigation system for providing the location of GPS receivers with great accuracy. Essentially it consists of a constellation of 24 high-altitude satellites orbiting the earth and the receivers on the surface of the planet which may be either stationary or in a moving vehicle (Spencer et al., 2003). Geodetic control provision is a branch of geodetic surveying that deals with the precise determination of the three-dimensional position of survey points on the surface of the earth. These points are from the primary control network for any surveying/mapping project. Conventionally, these points are determined by geodetic triangulation and astronomical observations. The density of these control points is further increased by triangulation, and EDM/Theodolite traverse. The advent of satellite technology has provided a new system known as Global Positioning System (GPS) designed by the U.S. Defense Department (Hoque, 2016). This system initially known as

"The Navigation Satellite Timing and Ranging" (NAVSTAR) is an all-weather satellite system primarily designed for navigation purposes. It is now utilised for providing the position of a point on the surface of the earth. Therefore, the GPS system is utilised nowadays as a modern surveying technique in the spheres of geodesy, surveying, and mapping.

PS receivers have been miniaturized to just a few integrated circuits and so are becoming very economical and that makes the technology accessible to virtually everyone. These days GPS is finding its way into cars, boats, planes, construction equipment, movie-making gear, farm machinery, cell phones, and even laptop computers. Currently, GPS is displaying its great utility in busting terrorist hideouts when wedded to missiles. It becomes a universal utility to mankind. GPS receivers have been miniaturized to just a few integrated circuits and so are becoming very economical and that makes the technology accessible to virtually everyone.

11.2 Components/segments of GPS

The GPS has several components, each of which represents impressive use of current, advanced technology and mathematics to bring it from trial stages up to today's stage where we all enjoy the benefits of outer space research and resources the US Department of Defense has committed to the program. The three components (Figure 11.1) of GPS are (a) Satellites Component, (b) Control Component, and (c) GPS User Component (Nikita et al., 2018). Terminology Used: The segment is the same as the Component.

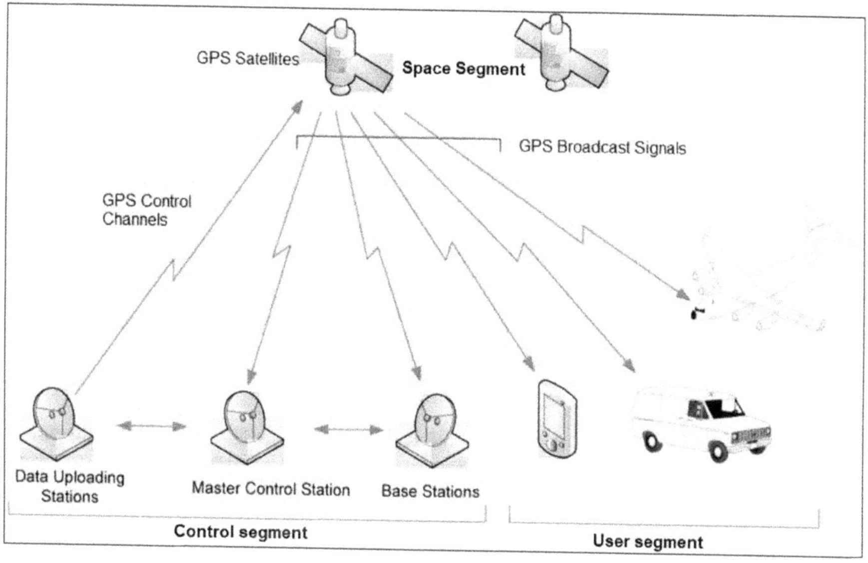

Figure 11.1 Three segments of GPS

11.2.1 Satellites Component

The GPS consists of a constellation of 24 satellites orbiting in highly inclined (polar) orbits, at altitudes around 20,200 km above the earth (Hoque, 2016). They continuously emit coded high-frequency radio signals which are received by GPS receivers and as well today by mobile phones due to the US Government's policy on free access to satellite signals for all mankind. These signals contain information about the exact orbits of the satellites and the precise time of atomic clocks onboard the satellites (Samama, 2008). When comparing the arrival times, the time delay between emission and receipt is measured and from the speed of light, just below 300,000 km/sec, the distance between the satellite and the receiver is computed.

Other basic characteristics of the Satellite Component are:

- At Altitude of 20200 km above the earth
- From the center of the earth approximately 26400 km
- Placed into Six (6) fixed orbital planes with 4 satellites to a plane
- Traveling speed of 3.87 km/sec

- The orbit period is almost 12 hours, less than 2 minutes every 12 hours (2 times a day)
- Orbital planes are equally spaced 60 degrees apart
- Inclined 55 degrees with respect to the equatorial plane
- Each satellite carries 3 atomic clocks, 2 rubidium, and 1 cesium
- 3 satellites are active spares that can replace failed satellites
- Increased number of satellites, the constellation was changed to a non-uniform arrangement. This showed improved reliability and availability of the system, relative to a uniform system when multiple satellites fail.
- Satellites repeat the same track/configuration over any point on earth every 24 hours (4 minutes earlier each day due to the earth's rotation around the sun)
- At any time there are 4 to 8 satellites 'visible' above 15° elevation and 10 visible satellites at an elevation of 10° from the location point of a receiver's antenna.

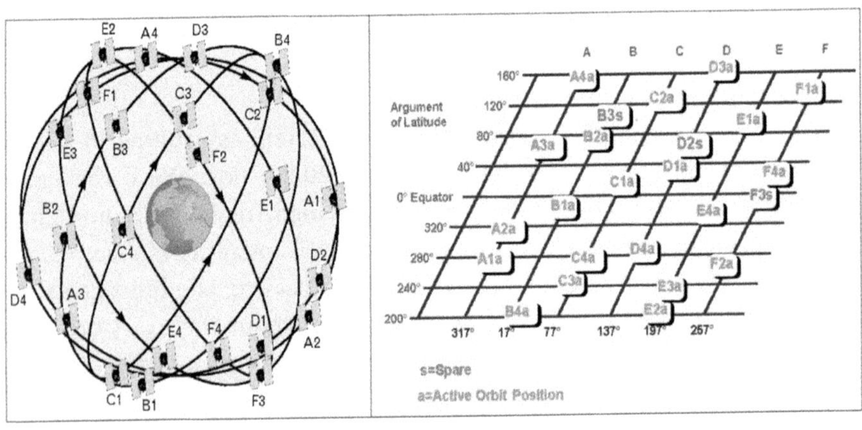

Figure 11.2 Constellation of twenty-four Global Positioning System (GPS) satellites in six orbital planes: (a) 3D orbital and (b) 2D orbital plane

11.2.2 Control Component

Ground stations are known as the "Control Segment" or "control component".These stations monitor the GPS satellites, checking both their operational health and their exact position in space. The master ground station transmits corrections for the satellite's ephemeris constants and clock offsets back to the satellites themselves. The satellites can then incorporate these updates in the signals they send to GPS receivers. The Control Segment consists of a system of tracking stations located around the world (Figure 11.3). The control segment consists of one Master Control Station (MCS) and five monitoring stations (Hoque, 2016). These five monitor stations are located in Hawaii, Ascension Island, Diego Garcia, Kwajalein, and Colorado Springs (Spencer et al., 2003).

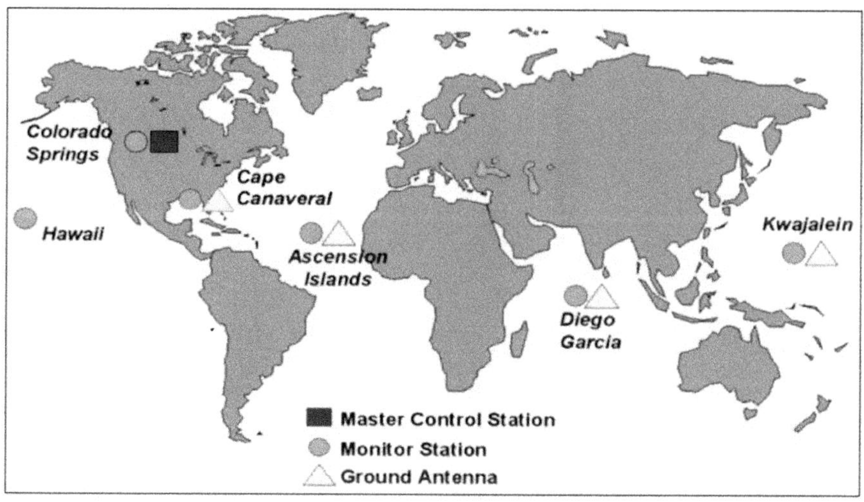

Figure 11.3 Location of Control Monitoring Stations

11.2.3 GPS User Component

The user segment is composed of hundreds of thousands of U.S. and allied military users of the secure GPS Precise Positioning Service, and tens of millions of civil, commercial, and scientific users of the Standard Positioning Service (Branford et al., 1996). In general, GPS receivers are composed of an antenna, tuned to the frequencies transmitted by the satellites, receiver-processors, and a highly stable clock. The User segment apart from the US and its Allies is the civilian with many applications including Surveying and Mapping. Anybody with GPS receivers is a User or the Mobile Phone those synchronises with GPS to update time, and as well provide GPS locations on mobile phones (Figure 11.4).

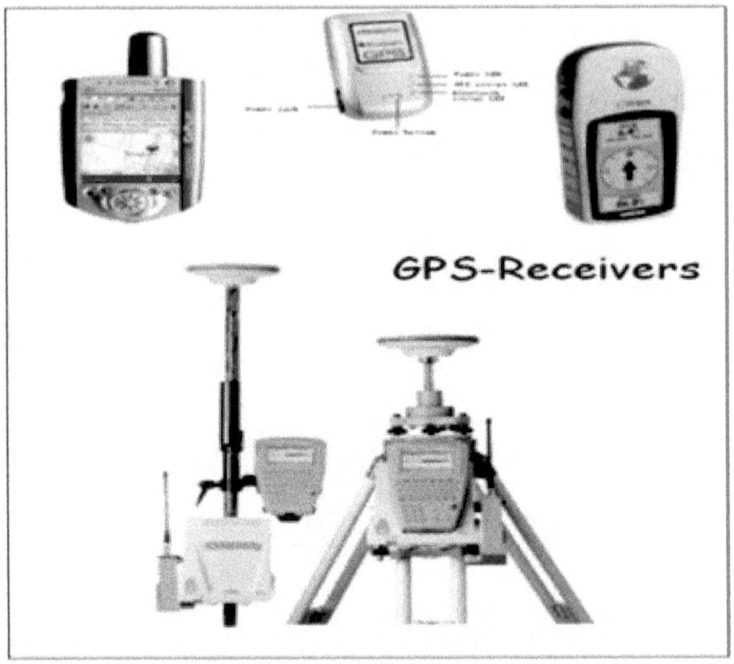

Figure 11.4 User components of GPS

11.3 Application of GPS

GPS applications are all those applications that use GPS to collect position, velocity, and time information to be used by the application (Branford et al., 1996). As stated by the US Government, the position and velocity provided by GPS may be used for civil applications such as:

Agriculture: GPS-based applications in precision farming are being used for farm planning, field mapping, soil sampling, tractor guidance, crop scouting, variable rate applications, and yield mapping.

Aviation Applications: GPS provides position determination for all phases of flight from departure, en route, and arrival, to airport surface navigation.

Rail Applications: Rail systems use the GPS in combination with other sensors to maintain a smooth flow of traffic, prevent collisions by precise knowledge of where a train is located, increase efficiency and capacity, etc.

Road Applications: GPS may be used to provide in-vehicle navigation, fleet management, tolling applications, etc.

Outdoor Navigation consists of the navigation in outdoor environments such as nature trails. Outdoor Navigation is used mainly by outdoor enthusiasts (such as hikers, backpackers, geocaching enthusiasts, mountaineers, or bikers) and outdoor workers (such as emergency workers, wildlife preservation workers, forestry workers, farmers, or mining workers).

Pedestrian Navigation or Road Navigation since it uses the concepts of trails and waypoints instead of a turn by turn navigation. Maps are not always required since individual trails can be loaded on the device or trails can be created from hikes. When present, maps are very different from the ones used in Pedestrian Navigation or Road Navigation; outdoor navigation maps are more closely related to topographic charts and military charts, rather than street and road-oriented.

Surveying and mapping: The main limitation of traditional surveying techniques is the requirement for a line of sight between surveying points. Using the accurate position provided by GPS surveying and mapping results can be obtained faster and at a lower cost.

Mobile Phones: The list of GPS applications is enormous and appreciated by the many users who depend so much on GPS such as on Navigation that it guarantees the user's safety with much economics of time and resources.

CHAPTER TWELVE

How GPS works-the basics of positioning

Learning Outcomes

On completion of this chapter students will be able to:

1. Understand basic positioning principles of GPS
2. Recognize pseudo-random code, ephemeris, dilution of Position (DOP), almanac in GPS
3. Evaluate the functionality of differential GPS.

12.1 Introduction to Positioning

The calculations used to determine your GPS receiver's position are based on very small time differences, from when the satellite transmitted the signal, to when the GPS receiver received the signal. These small differences are then used to calculate the distance from the receiver to the satellite. However, when receiving only one signal, we can only calculate how far away from the satellite we are. When receiving two signals, we can determine two likely positions where we are. We need three satellite signals to determine our exact position on the earth's surface (2D/ 2-dimensional positioning). When more than three satellites are 'visible' to the GPS receiver, it will also calculate the altitude of the receiver (3D/3 dimensional positioning).

The GPS receiver requires signals from at least three satellites to determine a unique position on the earth's surface. With a fourth signal, the altitude can also be determined. Receiving signals from more than four different satellites, the position of the GPS receiver can be more accurately determined.

GPS satellites carry atomic clocks that measure time to a high degree of accuracy (Grewal et al., 2007). The time information is placed in the codes broadcast by the satellite so that a receiver can continuously determine the time the signal was broadcast. The signal contains data that a receiver uses to compute the locations of the satellites and to make other adjustments needed for accurate positioning. The receiver uses the time difference between the time of signal reception and the broadcast time0 by the satellite to compute the range to the satellite. The receiver must account for propagation delays caused by the ionosphere and the troposphere. With three ranges to three satellites and knowing the location of the satellite when the signal was sent, the receiver can compute its three-dimensional position.

To compute ranges directly, however, the user must have an atomic clock synchronized to the global positioning system. By taking a measurement from an additional satellite, the receiver avoids the need for an atomic clock. The result is that the receiver uses a minimum of four satellites to compute latitude, longitude, altitude, and time.

12.2 Basic Positioning Principles of GPS - Trilateration

The basis of GPS is "trilateration" from satellites. Trilateration with GPS measures distances only from the satellites to one single receiver on or above the surface of the earth. A GPS receiver measures distance by measuring the transmission time of radio signals and determines the position of satellites with distance. It is a measurement of high orbit and precision positioning.

Suppose we measure our distance based on the difference of time from one satellite to any one receiver with the speed of light at 299,792,458 m per second, we find that we are anywhere on the surface of the earth with the radius of the distance measured from the satellite at some 20200 km from space.

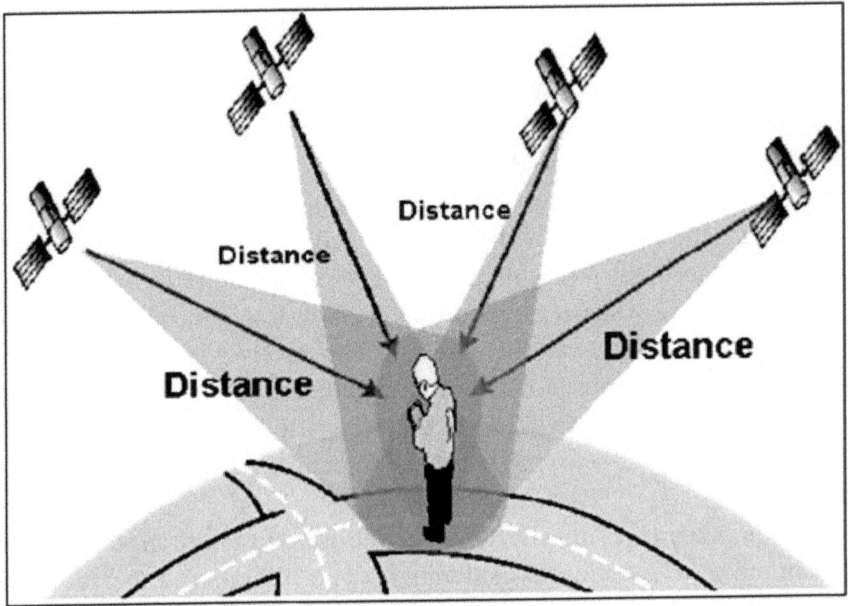

Figure 12.1 Process of Trilateration with Distances only

A second measurement taken from another satellite anywhere in space will approximately truncate to two possible places where the two circles of radius meet each other (Branford et al., 1996). Drawing circles with the satellites as the center will put our point location anywhere on any point on the surface of a sphere that is centered from two different locations of the two satellites that have a radius of 20200 km (Figure 12.2).

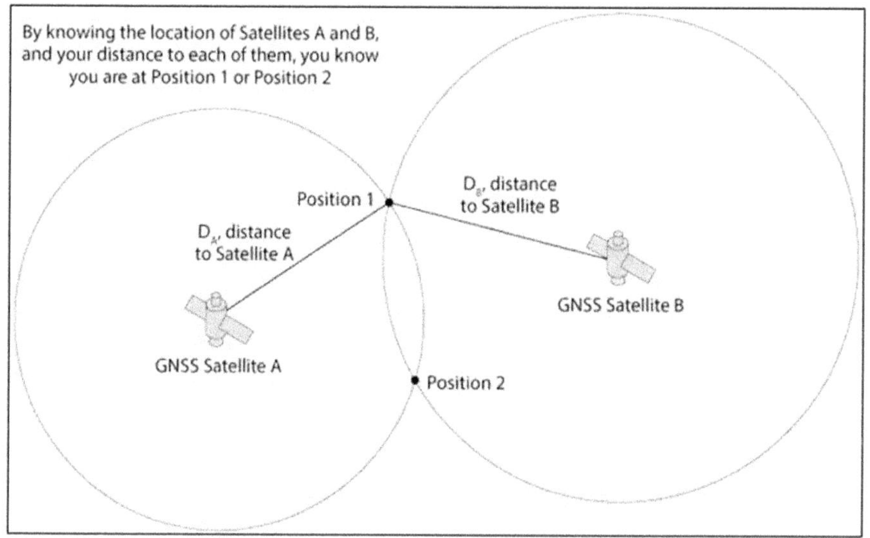

Figure 12.2 Trilateration (Ranging) from two Satellites

If we then make one more measurement from a third satellite, we surely can accurately within a couple of meters plot our position (static) on the surface of the earth. The third satellite has narrowed our position down even further, from the 2 possible points intersected by the two satellites sphere cuts through the circle that is the intersection of the first 2 spheres. So by ranging from 3 satellites we can narrow our position to just 2 points in space (Figure 12.3).

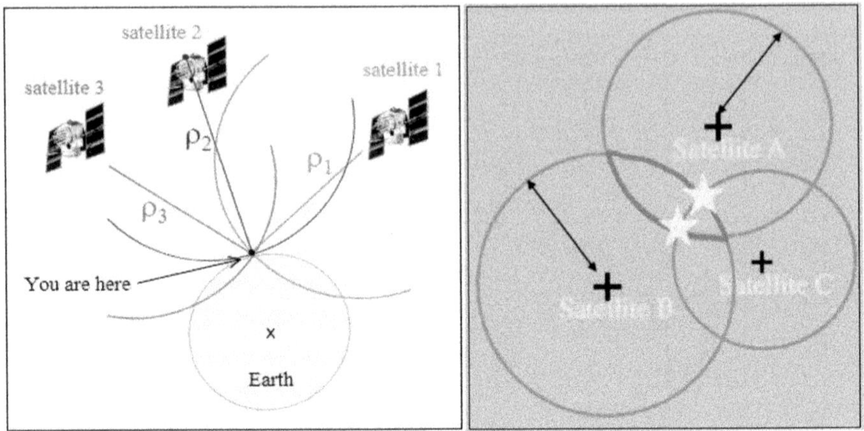

Figure 12.3 Trilateration (Ranging) from 3 Satellites

The practical solution of position determination is such that the satellites are well spaced in space, preferably within each quadrant of the sphere, and that the signal from satellites to the receiver travels through the same atmospheric condition, through the Ionosphere and the Troposphere. The delay signal is almost equal indicating that the elevation from the receiver is almost equal to within some 10° elevation above the GPS receiver. A much bigger error margin is expected where obstructions from satellites to the receiver are experienced by the user, and for this matter, the position quality is degraded. Many times locations are required besides tall buildings or in thick jungles and bush the satellite signal is obstructed physically, not the choice of the user (Spencer et al., 2003). The need to measure the distance from a fourth satellite is required to decide on which one is our true location (Figure 12.4).

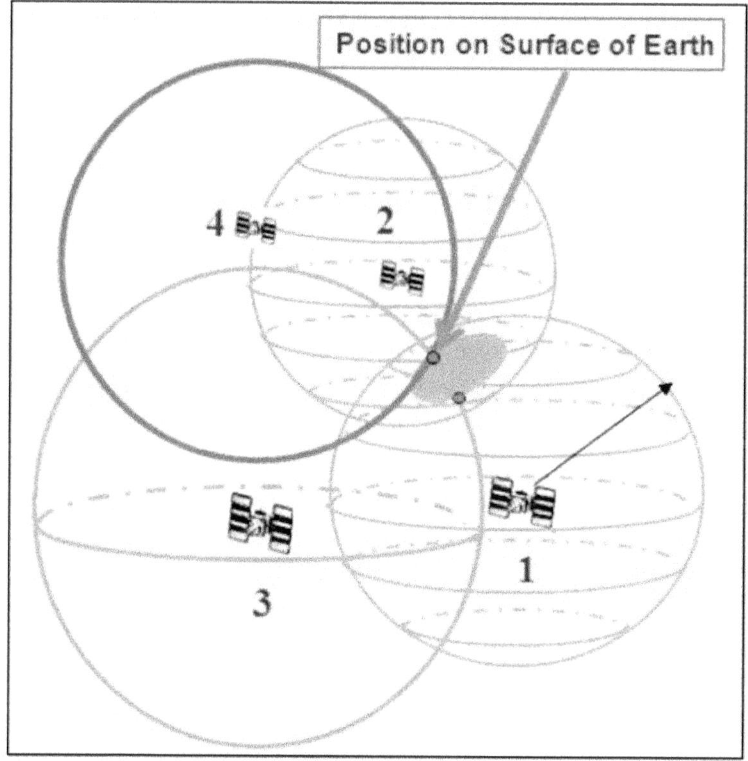

Figure 12.4 Trilateration (Ranging) from 4 Satellites

From the viewpoint of Physics, the product of signal transmission time x speed will be the distance between the satellite and the user. This distance is known as the virtual distance. In GPS measurement, we are measuring radio signals travel at quasi-light speed i.e. 299,792,458 meters per second. It is too fast that sometimes it takes only 0.06 seconds. Therefore, we need 2 timers: one on the satellite to record the signal sending time, and another one on the receiver to record the signal receiving time. Though the speed is fast, the signal sending/receiving time is not synchronous.

An approximation of delay time can be calculated knowing the satellite is 20,200 km away. The speed of light is 299,792,458 meters/second. The time of delay can be computed as:

20,200000m /299792458m/sec = 0.067 seconds as the time taken for the signal from satellite to the receiver. This is the basic theory of trilateration.

12.3 Pseudo random (PRN) code, ephemeris and almanac

GPS satellites send data that include the pseudo-random (PRN) code, ephemeris, and Almanac.

a. Pseudo-random code (how does GPS distance measuring code work for details) can help us find out the source satellite of signals. Therefore, it is also the ID code of a satellite, from 1 through 24. Therefore, we can see the satellite code from the GPS receiver. A PRN code is allocated for every single 24satellite in space.

b. Ephemeris data contain the status, current date, and time of the satellite. These allow your receiver to understand the current time and so to determine your present location.

c. Almanac transfers orbit data to inform the receiver of the location of each satellite in space.

Every satellite will tell your receiver 3 things: what satellite it is (pseudo-random code), where the satellite is (almanac), and when the message is sent (ephemeris). After receiving these data, the receiver will save the almanac and ephemeris data as a reference for time correction on the GPS receiver (Branford et al., 1996). After comparing the signal sending time of each satellite and the receiving time on the receiver, the receiver will calculate the distance between itself and each satellite. When receiving signals from more than one satellite, the receiver will triangulate the location. It needs 3 satellites to execute 2D positioning (latitude and longitude) and 4 or more satellites to execute 3D positioning (latitude, longitude, and altitude). By continually updating your locations, the receiver can locate your moving direction and speed.

12.4 Dilution of Position DOP

The satellite geometry will influence the accuracy of the GPS receiver. It refers to the relative position of individual satellites from the receiver. The angle of signal receiving will influence the accuracy of positioning. If the angle is too small, or the satellites are located too close to one another, the accuracy of positioning will be influenced. When the angle among satellites is small, a bigger error will occur (Figure 12.5).

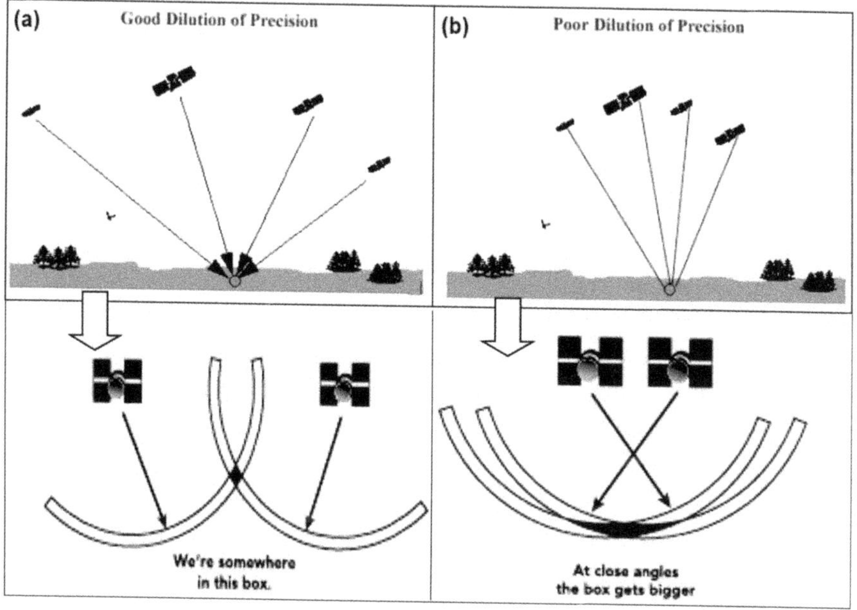

Figure 12.5 Satellite Spread - Dilution of Position: (a) Good DOP and (b) Poor DOP

Take 2 satellites for example, suppose satellites A and B are not moving in an instant, and that Satellite A is free from other interference and provides accurate positioning information. Errors occurred in Satellite B because SA is activated or there is other interference. The receiver will consider that the position of Satellite B is at the position of Satellite B1. When the adjacent angle of 2 satellites is big, the correction segment will be small, and the positioning will be more accurate. If 4 satellites are located in different directions, the positioning accuracy will be enhanced because the chances of signal intersection of these satellites will be very small.

12.5 How GPS works in five logical steps

1. The basis of GPS is "triangulation" from satellites.

1.2. One triangle formed from two satellites with one receiver on the ground produces one position.

1.3. Two triangles formed from three satellites with one single receiver on the ground produce three positions.

On that understanding, plenty more satellites that form a triangle mean plenty of positions to produce one good mean position on the ground.

2. To "triangulate," a GPS receiver measures distance using the travel time of radio signals.

3. To measure travel time, GPS needs very accurate timing, which it achieves with some tricks.

4. Along with distance, we need to know exactly where the satellites are in space. High orbits and careful monitoring are the secrets.

5. Finally we must correct for any delays the signal experiences as it travels through the atmosphere.

The same concept can be made simple as how surveyors measure bearings and distance from known coordinated points to compute coordinates of an unknown point. From many different known coordinated points to produce a good mean value of the intersection point.

Trilateration is a method of determining the relative positions of objects using the geometry of triangles in a similar fashion as triangulation. Unlike triangulation, which uses angle measurements (together with at least one known distance) to calculate the subject's location.

Trilateration on its own without coordinate origin is not valid when receivers are able to record coordinates, indicating that there is an original source of coordinates between the GPS receivers and the source (satellites). The known locations of two or more reference points and the measured distance between the subject and each reference point in order for Latitude and Longitude can be measured. Other factors affecting positioning accuracy include the ionosphere and troposphere in the atmosphere, internal clock error, and all other sources (El-Rabbany, 2002).

12.6 Intentional Errors!

As hard as it may be to believe, the same government that spent $12 Billion to develop the most accurate navigation system in the world is intentionally degrading its accuracy. The policy is called "Selective Availability" or "SA" and the idea behind it is to make sure that no hostile force or terrorist group can use GPS to make accurate weapons.

Basically, the DoD introduces some "noise" into the satellite's clock data which, in turn, adds noise (or inaccuracy) into position calculations. The DoD may also be sending slightly erroneous orbital data to the satellites, which they transmit back to receivers on the ground as part of a status message. Together these factors make SA the biggest single source of inaccuracy in the system. Military receivers use a decryption key to remove the SA errors and so they're much more accurate. Fortunately, all of these inaccuracies still don't add up to much of an error and a form of GPS called "Differential GPS" can significantly reduce these problems (Grewal et al., 2002).

12.7 Differential GPS

We will see how a simple concept can increase the accuracy of GPS to almost unbelievable limits. Basic GPS is the most accurate radio-based navigation system ever developed and for many applications, it's plenty accurate. But it's human nature to want MORE! So some crafty engineers came up with "Differential GPS," a way to correct the various inaccuracies in the GPS system, pushing its accuracy even further (Sabatini et al., 2008). Differential GPS or "DGPS" can yield measurements good to a couple of meters in moving applications and even better in stationary situations. That improved accuracy has a profound effect on the importance of GPS as a resource. With it, GPS becomes more than just a system for navigating boats and planes around the world. It becomes a universal measurement system capable of positioning things on a very precise scale.

Differential GPS involves the cooperation of two receivers, one that's stationary and another that's roving around making position measurements. The stationary receiver is the key. It ties all the satellite measurements into a solid local reference (Sabatini et al., 2008).

12.7.1 The problem

Remember that GPS receivers use timing signals from at least four satellites to establish a position. Each of those timing signals is going to have some error or delay depending on what sort of perils have befallen it on its trip down to us. Since each of the timing signals that go into a position calculation has some error, that calculation is going to be a compounding of those errors.

12.7.2 An extenuating circumstance

Luckily the sheer scale of the GPS system comes to our rescue. The satellites are so far out in space that the little distances we travel here on earth are insignificant. So if two receivers are fairly close to each other, say within a few hundred kilometers, the signals that reach both of them will have traveled through virtually the same slice of atmosphere, and so will have virtually the same errors.

12.7.3 The solution: reference receiver measures errors

The idea is simple. Put the reference receiver on a point that's been very accurately surveyed and keep it there. This reference station receives the same GPS signals as the roving receiver but instead of working like a normal GPS receiver, it attacks the equations backward. Instead of using timing signals to calculate its position, it uses its known position to calculate timing. It figures out what the travel time of the GPS signals should be, and compares it with what they actually are. The difference is an "error correction" factor.

The receiver then transmits this error information to the roving receiver so it can use it to correct its measurements (Branford et al., 1996).

12.7.4 Reference receiver catalogs all satellites

Since the reference receiver has no way of knowing which of the many available satellites a roving receiver might be used to calculate its position, the reference receiver quickly runs through all the visible satellites and computes each of their errors (Sabatini et al., 2008). Then it encodes this information into a standard format and transmits it to the roving receivers (Figure 12.6).

It's as if the reference receiver is saying: "OK everybody, right now the signal from satellite #1 is ten nanoseconds delayed, satellite #2 is three nanoseconds delayed, and satellite #3 is sixteen nanoseconds delayed...." and so on. The roving receivers get the complete list of errors and apply the corrections for the particular satellites they're using.

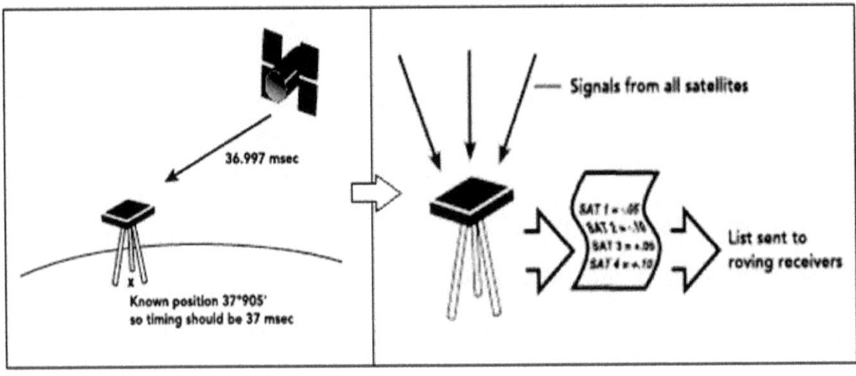

Figure 12.6 Reference receiver and error transmission for its correction

12.8 Applications of GPS in Geoinformatics

- ***Mapping with Satellite Images: Satellite*** images are nowadays, widely employed for a large number of mapping projects including Topographic

Surveys and Thematic Mapping (Hoque, 2016). The original image data suffers from a number of geometric distortions due to variations in altitude, attitude, etc. of the satellite at the time of imaging. Therefore, this data needs some pre-processing in order to bring back the geometric fidelity. Usually, a number of GCPs (points whose coordinates with respect to a mapping reference system are known and whose image coordinates are observable) are utilised for implementing the corrections on the image data. Here, GPS technology plays a significant role.

- ***Topographic Mapping:*** The GPS technology can be utilised in topographic mapping for the provision of Ground Control points.
- ***Cadastral Surveying:*** Cadastral Maps are large-scale maps on scales varying between 1:500 to 1:8,000 depicting property boundary lines. Conventionally, the survey for this is carried out by ground survey methods using theodolites or EDM (Electro-magnetic Distance Measurement) instruments. The aerial photogrammetric techniques are also used now a day with limited ground control points from cited ground survey methods. The GPS technology here offers an efficient tool for directly surveying on the ground. Also, this can be utilised for control provision for aerial photogrammetric methods.
- ***Town Planning & Engineering Surveys:*** GPS is now extensively used to record the track of a new road for inclusion on a map in a town planning survey. It is being used to position a drill bit over a particular spot on the ocean floor from a pitching boat. There are many more applications needing precise fixing of positions.
- ***GIS Applications:*** GPS is a powerful tool to support a GIS (Geographic Information System). Its role is enumerated below:

- It contributes to a uniform basic geometric frame, for example, a co-ordinate system, a digital map, or a digital terrain model.
- It contributes to the geometric location of objects that enter the GIs. For example streets, buildings, power lines, property boundaries, etc.
- It allows GIS to be taken out into the field with GPS direct entry.

Depending on accuracy requirements GPS provides continuous position information for all scales of interest. Therefore, the integration of GPS technology with GIS is the state of the art.

References

1. Branford, W., Parkinson, J., and Spilker, J. (1996). Global Positioning System: Theory and Applications, volume.1, Amer Inst of Aeronautics, Lincoln, NE, U.S.A.
2. Burrough, P.A., and McDonnell, R.A. (2015). Principles of Geographic Information Systems, 2nd ed., Oxford University Press, Oxford. ISBN: 978-0-198-23365-7.
3. Campbell, J.B., and Wynne, R. H. (2011). Introduction to Remote Sensing. The Guilford Press, New York, ISBN: 978-1-609-18176-5
4. CASA (2006). Civil Aviation Advisory Publication 179A-1(1). Navigation using Global Navigation Satellite Systems (GNSS) Canberra.
5. CCRS (2009).Fundamentals of Remote Sensing, Canada Centre for Remote Sensing, 2009.
6. Chang, K.T. (2018). Introduction to geographic information systems, 9th ed., McGraw-Hill, ISBN: 978-1-259-92964-9
7. Chraibi, M., Seyfried, A., and Schadschneider, A. (2010). Generalized centrifugal-force model for pedestrian dynamics, Physical Review, E82, 046111.
8. Clarke, K. C. (1995). Analytical and Computer Cartography, 2nd ed., Englewood Cliffs, New Jearsey, Prentice Hall, ISBN: 978-0-130-33481-7.
9. Cleland, D. T., Avers, R. E., McNab, W. H., Jensen, M. E., Bailey, R. G., King, T. and Russell, W. E. (1997). National Hierarchical Framework of Ecological Units. In Boyce, M. S. and Hancy, A., eds., Ecosystem Management Applications for Sustainable Forest and Wildlife Resources, New Haven, CT: Yale University Press, pp. 181–200.
10. Cooke, D. F. (1998). Topology and TIGER: The Census Bureau's Contribution, In Foresman, T. W. (ed.), The History of Geographic Information Systems: Perspectives from the Pioneers, pp. 47–57.Upper Saddle River, New Jersey, Prentice Hall.
11. Curtis H. D. (2010). Orbital Mechanics for Engineering Students, Butterworth-Heinemann, ISBN: 978-0-123-74778-5.
12. Dangermond, J. (1982). A Classification of Software Components Commonly Used in Geographic Information Systems, In *Proceedings of the U.S.-Australia Workshop on the Design and Implementation of Computer-Based Geographic Information Systems*, 70–91.

13. DeMers, M. N.(1997). Fundamentals of Geographic Information Systems, Wiley, ISBN: 978-0-471-14284-3
14. El-Rabbany, A. (2002). Introduction to GPS: The Global Positioning System, Artech House, ISBN: 978-1-580-53183-2.
15. Environmental Systems Research Institute, Inc. (1998). Understanding GIS: The ARC/INFO Method, 4th ed., Redlands, CA: ESRI Press, ISBN: 978-1-879-10201-9.
16. Goodchild, M. F. (2002). GIS and basic research: The national center for geographic information and analysis, Government Information Quarterly, 7(3), 343-355
17. Grewal, M.S., Weill, L.R., and Andrews, A.P. (2007). Global Positioning Systems, Inertial Navigation, and Integration, 2nd Ed., Wiley-Interscience, ISBN: 978-0-470-04190-1.
18. Hoque, Z. (2016). Basic Concept of GPS and Its Applications, IOSR Journal of Humanities and Social Science, 21 (3), 31-37.
19. Lillesand, T., Kiefer, R. W., and Chipman, J. (2015) Remote Sensing and Image Interpretation, 7th Edn., Wiley and Sons ISBN: 978-1-118-34328-9
20. Longley, P. A., Goodchild, M.F., Maguire, D.J., and Rhind, D.W. (2015). Geographic Information Systems and Science, 4th ed., John Wiley and Sons Ltd, Chichester, ISBN: 978-1-118-67695-0.
21. Nikita, K., Urmil D., Shwet,a J., and Akansha, B. (2018). Global Positioning System, International Journal of Engineering Research & Technology, 6(12), 1-3.
22. Nyerges, T. L. (1990). Locational Referencing and Highway Segmentation in a Geographic Information System. ITE Journal, 60:27–31.
23. Oz, E. (2004). Management Information Systems, 4th ed. Boston, MA: Course Technology, ISBN: 978-0-619-21538-5.
24. Russell, J. L. (1964). Kepler's Laws of Planetary Motion: 1609-1666. The British Journal for the History of Science, 2(1), 1–24. http://www.jstor.org/stable/4025081
25. Sabatini, R., Palmerini, G. B., & North Atlantic Treaty Organization. (2008). Differential global positioning system (DGPS) for flight testing. Neuilly-sur-Seine Cedex, France: North Atlantic Treaty Organization, Research and Technology Organization.
26. Samama, N. (2008). Global Positioning: Technologies and Performance. John Wiley & Sons, ISBN978-0-470-24190-5.
27. Spencer, J., Frizzelle, B. G., Page, P. H. and Vogler, J.B. (2003). Global

Positioning System: a field guide for the social sciences. London: Blackwell Publishers, ISBN: 978-1-405-10185-1.

28. Star, J., and Estes, J. (1990). Geographic information systems: an introduction, Prentice-Hall, Englewood Cliffs, New Jersey, ISBN:978-0-133-51123-9
29. Stevens, S. S. (1946). On the Theory of Scales of Measurement. Science, 103:677–80.
30. Wilson, R. J., and Watkins, J. J. (1991). Graphs: An Introductory Approach, New York, Wiley, ISBN: 978-0-471-61554-5.

www.ingramcontent.com/pod-product-compliance
Ingram Content Group UK Ltd.
Pitfield, Milton Keynes, MK11 3LW, UK
UKHW021915190726
13853UKWH00002B/681

9 798889 516965